The
Knitter's
Year

The Knitter's Year

52 MAKE-IN-A-WEEK PROJECTS—
QUICK GIFTS AND SEASONAL
KNITS

DEBBIE BLISS

PHOTOGRAPHY BY PENNY WINCER

TRAFALGAR SQUARE
North Pomfret, Vermont

In memory of my wonderful mother, Mid.

When it comes to knitting, in my mind there is an immense amount of pleasure to be gained from picking up a project that can be easily completed in a short amount of time. With most of us contending with busy, if not frantic lifestyles, when we do manage to carve out a small amount of time, it is often all too brief. But these short spells of downtime can be the perfect moments to craft something that demands very little from us apart from a pair of needles, a small quantity of yarn, and an equal amount of enthusiasm.

With this in mind, I have created *The Knitter's Year*. This book offers 52 designs to take you all the way from spring through to the winter months. The projects are set within the different seasons, including fingerless gardening gloves to entice you outside in spring, the perfect beach bag to get you set for summer, a pair of cozy slippers to keep you warm as the weather turns to fall and, finishing the year, is a wintry hot-water bottle cover and festive holiday decorations. The projects are of varying complexity but each one is designed to be able to be completed within one week or even less. Similarly, the ideas range in scale from a winter-warmer scarf that takes seven balls of yarn to a cute Easter bunny egg cozy and a floral corsage, which are both made from only small amounts of leftover yarn and so can help you to use up your yarn stash.

I hope you enjoy the designs in *The Knitter's Year*, both to make for yourself and to give as special handmade gifts. Why not give your home a fresh look with the gingham pillow or decorative lace shelf edging? Or how about making the pumpkin pincushion or sewing needle case for a crafter friend? Or send your child back to school with their own unique pencil case to make the new fall term a little brighter?

As with all my work, none of it would be possible without the huge support I get from great knitters, editors, and pattern checkers, but I can honestly say that *The Knitter's Year* would not have come to fruition without the invaluable contribution of Rosy Tucker. Friend and colleague, she was there from the initial brainstorming and scribbling of lists in cafés, continuing with her design and practical input to the collection. I love the sheer joy of collaborating with other people and feel privileged to not only have had the opportunity to work once more with Rosy but also the fantastic team at Quadrille Publishing.

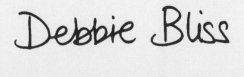

Types of yarn

The yarns I have chosen for the designs in this book range from my organic cottons to cashmerinos and pure wools, each with their own contribution to make to the designs. It may be that they give crisp stitch detail in a simple pattern, such as the textured basket worked in aran-weight cotton, or provide softness and coziness in a chunky scarf.

Unless you are using up your stash to make the smaller items in this book, make the effort to buy the yarn stated in the pattern. Each of these designs has been created with a specific yarn in mind.

A different yarn may not produce the same quality of fabric or have the same wash-and-wear properties. From an aesthetic point of view, the clarity of a subtle stitch pattern may be lost if a garment is knitted in an inferior yarn. However, there may be occasions when a knitter needs to substitute a yarn—if there is an allergy to wool, for example—and so the following is a guideline to making the most informed choices.

Always buy a yarn that is the same weight as that given in the pattern: replace a double knitting with a double knitting, for example, and check that the gauge of both yarns is the same.

Where you are substituting a different fiber, be aware of the design. A cable pattern knitted in cotton when worked in wool will pull in because of the greater elasticity of the yarn and so the fabric will become narrower; this will alter the proportions of the garment.

Check the length of the yarn ball. Yarns that weigh the same may have different lengths in the ball or hank, so you may need to buy more or less yarn.

Here are descriptions of my yarns and a guide to their weights and types:

Debbie Bliss Baby Cashmerino:
- A fine-weight yarn (between a fingering-weight and a double-knitting-weight).
- 55% merino wool, 33% microfiber, 12% cashmere.
- Approximately 137yd per 1¾oz/50g ball.

Debbie Bliss Cashmerino Aran:
- An aran-weight yarn.
- 55% merino wool, 33% microfiber, 12% cashmere.
- Approximately 99yd per 1¾oz/50g ball.

Debbie Bliss Como:
- A super-bulky-weight yarn.
- 90% wool, 10% cashmere.
- Approximately 46yd per 1¾oz/50g ball.

Debbie Bliss Cotton DK:
- A double-knitting-weight yarn.
- 100% cotton.
- Approximately 92yd per 1¾oz/50g ball.

Debbie Bliss Eco Aran:
- An aran-weight yarn.
- 100% organic cotton.
- Approximately 99yd per 1¾oz/50g ball.

Debbie Bliss Eco Baby:
- A fine-weight yarn (between a fingering-weight and a double-knitting weight).
- 100% organic cotton.
- Approximately 137yd per 1¾oz/50g ball.

Debbie Bliss Fez:
- An aran-weight yarn.
- 85% extra-fine merino wool, 15% camel.
- Approximately 110yd per 1¾oz/50g ball.

Debbie Bliss Rialto 4-Ply:
- A fingering-weight yarn.
- 100% extra-fine merino wool.
- Approximately 110yd per 1¾oz/50g ball.

Debbie Bliss Rialto Aran:
- An aran-weight yarn.
- 100% extra-fine merino wool.
- Approximately 88yd per 1¾oz/50g ball.

Debbie Bliss Rialto DK:
- A double-knitting-weight yarn.
- 100% extra-fine merino wool.
- Approximately 115yd per 1¾oz/50g ball.

BUYING YARN

The yarn label on the yarn will carry all the essential information you need as to recommended gauge, needle size, weight, and yardage. Importantly it will also have the dye-lot number. Yarns are dyed in batches or lots, which can vary considerably. As your yarn store may not have the same dye lot later on, buy all your yarn for a project at the same time. If you know that sometimes you use more yarn than that specified in the pattern, buy extra. If it is not possible to buy all the yarn you need with the same dye-lot number, use the different ones where it will not show as much, on a neck or border, as a change of dye lot across a main piece will be more likely to show.

It is also a good idea at the time of buying the yarn to check the pattern and make sure that you already have the needles you will require. If not, buy them now, as it will save a lot of frustration when you get home.

ABBREVIATIONS

In a pattern book general abbreviations will usually be given at the front before the patterns begin, while those more specific to a particular design will be given at the start of the individual pattern. The following are the ones used throughout this book.

STANDARD ABBREVIATIONS

alt	alternate
beg	begin(ning)
cont	continu(e)(ing)
dec	decreas(e)(ing)
DK	double knitting (a standard UK yarn weight)
foll	follow(s)(ing)
garter st	garter stitch (k every row)
in	inch(es)
inc	increas(e)(ing)
k	knit
kfb	knit into front and back of next stitch
M1	make one stitch by picking up the loop lying between the stitch just worked and the next stitch and working into the back of it
oz	ounce(s)
patt	pattern; or work in pattern
p	purl
psso	pass slipped stitch over
rem	remain(s)(ing)
rep	repeat(s)(ing)
skp	slip 1, knit 1, psso
sl	slip
ssk	[slip 1 knitwise] twice, insert tip of left-hand needle from left to right through fronts of slipped stitches and k2tog
st(s)	stitch(es)
st st	stockinette stitch
tbl	through back loop(s)
tog	together
yd	yard(s)
yo	yarn over (yarn around right-hand needle to make a new stitch)

Spring

Basket

For those in need of extra storage space, this charming knitted basket makes both a stylish and practical option. Worked in a textured knit and purl stitch using a crisp cotton yarn, the finished knitted fabric is lined and stiffened to achieve its rectangular shape. To complement the chocolate brown yarn, I have used a classic blue ticking stripe as the lining fabric for the basket.

SIZE
7in tall x 10¾in wide x
7in deep

MATERIALS
Debbie Bliss Eco Aran (100%
organic cotton, approx 99 yd
per 1¾oz/50g ball)
Four balls in chocolate brown
Pair of size 7 knitting needles
39½in x 12in piece of buckram
26½in x 22¾in piece of cotton
fabric for lining

GAUGE
18 sts and 30 rows to 4in
square over patt using size
7 needles.

ABBREVIATIONS
See page 10.

NOTE
Basket is made in one piece.

TO MAKE
With size 7 needles, cast on 49 sts.
1st row (right side) K1, [p1, k1] to end.
2nd row P to end.
3rd row P1, [k1, p1] to end.
4th row P to end.
These 4 rows **form** the patt and are repeated.
Patt 2 rows.
** Front handle
Next row (right side) Patt 16, turn and cont on these sts only for first side of handle.
Patt 5 rows on these 16 sts, so ending with a p row, leave sts on a holder.
Next row With right side facing, rejoin yarn to rem 33 sts, bind off 17 sts, patt to end.
Patt 5 rows.
Next row (wrong side) P16, cast on 17 sts, p16 sts from holder. *49 sts.* **
Work even in patt until front measures 7in from cast-on edge, ending with a right-side row.
Foldline row (wrong side) K to end.
Shape for sides and base
Next row Cast on 34 sts, patt to end. *83 sts.*
Next row Cast on 34 sts, p to end. *117 sts.*

Cont in patt until work measures 14in from original cast-on edge, ending with a p row.
Shape for back
Next row Bind off 34 sts, patt to end. *83 sts.*
Foldline row Bind off 34 sts, k to end. *49 sts.*
Cont in patt until work measures 19½in, ending with a wrong-side row.
Back handle
Work as Front handle from ** to **.
Work 5 rows more in patt, so ending with a right-side row.
Bind off knitwise.

a smart, all-purpose
storage solution

TO FINISH

From interlining, cut two pieces 7in square for ends and three pieces 7in x 10¾in for sides and base. Cut out the handle slots in the two side pieces. Attach the interling pieces to the knitted piece; if your interling has an iron-on adhesive side, iron in place, otherwise sew in place. Fold up the knitted piece and sew together the edges.

LINING

From the fabric piece, cut out four 7¼in squares, one from each corner, so leaving a cross shape. Fold up the fabric (use the knitted piece as a guide), then taking ⅝in seam allowances, sew together the sides of the cross. Make a cut in the fabric sides for the center of the handles, snipping out from the ends of the cut to the corners of the handle (see above right), fold the cut fabric onto the wrong side and press in

place to neaten the handle. Press ¾in onto the wrong side around the top edge, place the lining in the basket and slipstitch in place around the handles and top edge.

HANDLE CUT-OUT

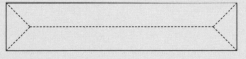

KEY
---- cutting line

Lace pillow

As the days get warmer and longer, a crisp white cotton pillow provides perfect comfort when lounging outside in the spring sunshine. The cable and lace panel is knitted first and then sewn onto an existing pillow cover; I have contrasted the white lace panel against a charcoal gray pillow for maximum impact while the knitting is kept to a minimum. Making this project is a great way to practice your lacework skills as, unlike knitting a garment, you don't have to worry about shaping at the same time.

SIZE
Approximately 16½in square

MATERIALS
Debbie Bliss Eco Aran (100% organic cotton, approx 99 yd per 1¾oz/50g ball)
Two balls in white
Pair of size 7 knitting needles
Cable needle
18in square fabric pillow cover and pillow form

GAUGE
19 sts and 25 rows to 4in square over St st using size 7 needles.

ABBREVIATIONS
C3F slip next 2 sts onto cable needle and hold to front of work, k1, then k2 from cable needle.
C3B slip next st onto cable needle and hold at back of work, k2, then k1 from cable needle.
C3BP slip next st onto cable needle and hold at back of work, k2, then p1 from cable needle.
C3FP slip next 2 sts onto cable needle and hold to front of work, p1, then k2 from cable needle.
C4B slip next 2 sts onto cable needle and hold at back of work, k2, then k2 from cable needle.
C4F slip next 2 sts onto cable needle and hold to front of work, k2, then k2 from cable needle.
sk2p slip 1, k2tog, pass slipped st over the k2tog.
Also see page 10.

PANEL PATTERN A
Worked over 19 sts.
1st row (right side) K1, [yo, ssk] 3 times, k5, [k2tog, yo] 3 times, k1.
2nd and every foll wrong-side row Purl.
3rd row K2, [yo, ssk] 3 times, k3, [k2tog, yo] 3 times, k2.
5th row K3, [yo, ssk] 3 times, k1, [k2tog, yo] 3 times, k3.
7th row K4, [yo, ssk] twice, yo, sk2p, yo, [k2tog, yo] twice, k4.
9th row K5, [yo, ssk] twice, yo, sk2p, yo, k2tog, yo, k5.
11th row K6, [yo, ssk] twice, yo, sk2p, yo, k6.
13th row K7, [yo, ssk] 3 times, k6.
15th row K5, k2tog, yo, k1, [yo, ssk] 3 times, k5.
17th row K4, [k2tog, yo] twice, k1, [yo, ssk]

19

3 times, k4.

19th row K3, [k2tog, yo] 3 times, k1, [yo, ssk] 3 times, k3.

21st row K2, [k2tog, yo] 3 times, k3, [yo, ssk] 3 times, k2.

23rd row K1, [k2tog, yo] 3 times, k5, [yo, ssk] 3 times, k1.

24th row Purl.

These 24 rows **form** Patt Panel A and are repeated.

PANEL PATTERN B

Worked over 17 sts.

1st row (right side) P1, C3FP, k2tog, yo, k3, yo, ssk, k1, C3F, p2.

2nd row K2, p13, k2.

3rd row P2, C3FP, k2, k2tog, yo, k1, yo, ssk, k1, C3F, p1.

4th row K1, p13, k3.

5th row P2, C3B, k1, k2tog, yo, k3, yo, ssk, C3BP, p1.

6th row K2, p13, k2.

7th row P1, C3B, k1, k2tog, yo, k1, yo, ssk, k2, C3BP, p2.

8th row K3, p13. k1.

These 8 rows **form** Patt Panel B and are repeated.

PILLOW FRONT

With size 7 needles, cast on 77 sts.

Seed st row K1, [p1, k1] to end.

Rep this row 5 times more.

Foundation row (wrong side) Seed st 5, p19, k1, p4, k4, p13, k2, p4, k1, p19, seed st 5.

Now work in patt as follows:

1st row (right side) Seed st 5, work across 19 sts of 1st row of Patt A, p1, C4B, p1, work across 17 sts of 1st row of Patt B, p1, C4F, p1, work across 19 sts of 1st row of Patt A, seed st 5.

2nd row Seed st 5, work across 19 sts of 2nd row of Patt A, k1, p4, k1, work across 17 sts of 2nd row of Patt B, k1, p4, k1, work across 19 sts of 2nd row of Patt A, seed st 5.

3rd row (right side) Seed st 5, work across 19 sts of 3rd row of Patt A, p1, k4, p1, work across 17 sts of 3rd row of Patt B, p1, k4, p1, work across 19 sts of 3rd row of Patt A, seed st 5.

4th row Seed st 5, work across 19 sts of 4th row of Patt A, k1, p4, k1, work across 17 sts of 4th row of Patt B, k1, p4, k1, work across 19 sts of 4th row of Patt A, seed st 5.

These 4 rows **form** the two 4-st cables and set the position of the Patt Panels.

Working correct patt panel rows, cont in patt until 3 repeats of the 24 rows of Patt Panel A have been worked, so ending with a wrong-side row.

Work 5 rows in seed st.

Bind off in seed st.

TO FINISH

Position the knitted piece centrally on the pillow cover front and slipstitch in place around the edge. Insert pillow form.

Flowerpot covers

Do your floral arrangements need brightening up for spring? Then why not knit some decorative pot covers in delicate seasonal pastels? Seed stitch in leaf green, stockinette stitch in pale pink, and a fine cable rib in pale blue echo the shades of springtime blooms. All three covers are worked in simple stitches, which make them quick and easy to make up.

SIZE

Approximately 2¾in high to fit 4–4¼in diameter terracotta flowerpots

MATERIALS

Debbie Bliss Cotton DK (100% organic cotton, approx 92 yd per 1¾oz/50g ball)
One ball in each of pale pink, apple green, and duck egg
Pair of size 6 knitting needles
Cable needle (optional)

GAUGE

20 sts and 28 rows over St st and 20 sts and 32 rows over seed st, both to 4in square using size 6 needles.

ABBREVIATIONS

C2B slip next st onto cable needle and hold at back of work, k1, then k1 from cable needle or if working without the cable needle, k into front of 2nd st on left-hand needle, then k into front of 1st st and slip both sts off needle together. Also see page 10.

RIB AND MOCK CABLE COVER

With size 6 needles and duck egg, cast on 46 sts.
1st row P2, [k2, p2] to end.
2nd row K2, [p2, k2] to end.
3rd row P2, [C2B, p2, k2, p2], to last 4 sts, C2B, p2.
4th row Rep 2nd row.
These 4 rows **form** the basic patt and are repeated.
Keeping patt correct and taking inc sts into k2, p2 rib, work 18 rows more and inc 1 st at each end of 1st, 4th, 7th, 10th, and 13th rows. *56 sts.*
Bind off in patt.

TO FINISH

Sew seam and place around flowerpot.

STOCKINETTE STITCH COVER

With size 6 needles and pale pink, cast on 39 sts. Beg with a k row, work 22 rows in St st and inc 1 st at each end of 3rd, 6th, 9th, 12th, 15th, and 18th rows. *51 sts.*
Bind off.

TO FINISH

Sew seam and place around flowerpot.

SEED STITCH COVER

With size 6 needles and apple green, cast on 39 sts.
Seed st row K1, [p1, k1] to end.
Rep this row 23 times more and taking inc sts into seed st, inc 1 st at each end of 3rd, 6th, 9th, 12th, 15th, and 18th rows. *51 sts.*
Bind off in seed st.

TO FINISH

Sew seam and place around flowerpot.

pretty pastel
pot covers

Floral corsage

When I embarked on my career as a knitwear designer, I started out making hand-knitted plants so this floral corsage is a return to my design roots! If you are looking for a quick way to perk up an outfit, try this pretty rose in delicate shades of pink. For more of an impact, work the rose in vivid shades such as deep crimson with fuchsia or violet and mauve.

SIZE
Approximately 3¼in x 2¼in
(including leaves)

MATERIALS
Debbie Bliss Cotton DK
(100% organic cotton, approx
92 yd per 1¾oz/50g ball)
Small amount in each of rose
pink (A), pale pink (B), and
apple green (C)
Pair each of sizes 5 and 7
knitting needles
Brooch pin

ABBREVIATIONS
See page 10.

OUTER PETAL (MAKE 1)
With size 7 needles and A, cast on 81 sts.
K 1 row.
Next row P2, [k1, slip this st back on left-hand needle, lift next 10 sts one at a time over this st and off left-hand needle, slip st back onto right-hand needle] to last 2 sts, p2.
K 1 row.
Cut yarn and thread through rem 11 sts, pull tightly to gather, and secure.

ROSE CENTER (MAKE 1)
With size 7 needles and B, cast on 15 sts.
Beg with a k row, work 4 rows in St st.
Picot row (right side) With A, [k2tog, yo] to end.
Beg with a p row, work 4 rows in St st.
Bind off.
Fold in half along picot row and sew cast-on to bound-off edge.

Sew together row-end edges.
Roll the strip around itself to form the rose center and stitch to secure.

LEAVES (MAKE 2)
With size 5 needles and C, cast on 8 sts.
P 1 row.
Next row Skp, k to last 2 sts, k2tog.
Rep the last 2 rows once more. *4 sts.*
P 1 row.
Next row Skp, k2tog. *2 sts.*
P 1 row.
Next row K2tog and fasten off.

TO FINISH
Stitch rose center in place to the center of the outer petal. Arrange the leaves behind the flower and stitch in place. Sew a brooch pin to back.

a darling
rosebud brooch

Washcloth

Knitted in my Eco Baby yarn—a Fairtrade organic cotton—this textured washcloth takes less than an hour to make. Worked in reversible seed stitch with a garter stitch edge, the finished cloth can be used as a washcloth while bathing or as a dishcloth; either way, it couldn't be easier.

SIZE
Approximately 10in square

MATERIALS
Debbie Bliss Eco Baby (100% organic cotton, approx 137 yd per 1¾oz/50g ball)
One ball in duck egg
Pair of size 3 knitting needles

GAUGE
25 sts and 38 rows to 4in square over seed st using size 3 needles.

ABBREVIATIONS
See page 10.

TO MAKE
With size 3 needles, cast on 63 sts.
K 6 rows.
Next row (right side) K5, [p1, k1] to last 4 sts, k4.
Next row K4, [p1, k1] to last 5 sts, p1, k4.
Next row K4, [p1, k1] to last 5 sts, p1, k4.
Next row K5, [p1, k1] to last 4 sts, k4.
The last 4 rows **form** seed st with garter st borders and are repeated.
Cont in patt until cloth measures 9in from cast-on edge, ending with a wrong-side row.
K 6 rows.
Bind off.

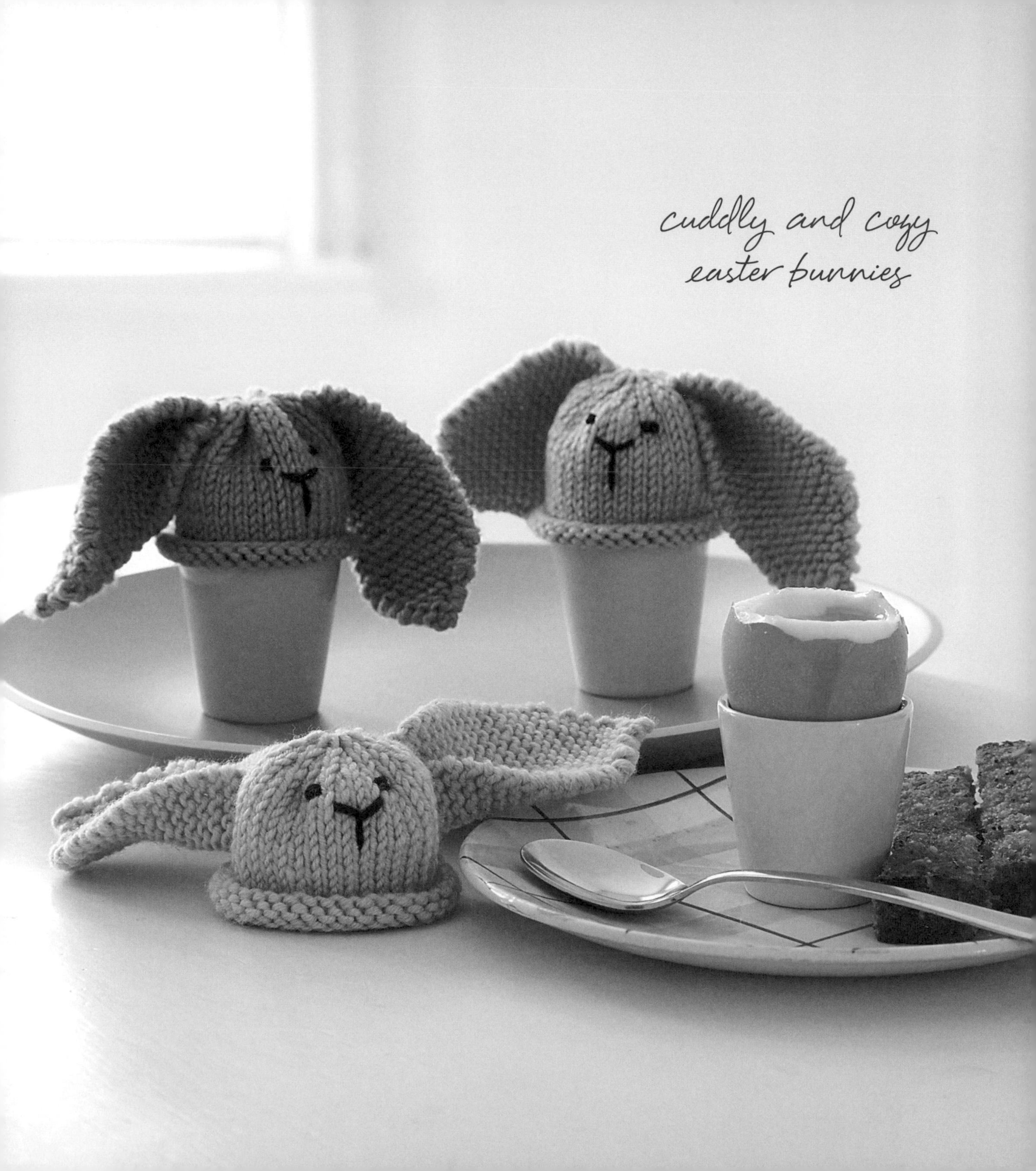

cuddly and cozy
easter bunnies

Bunny egg cozies

Keep your boiled eggs warm at Easter, and beyond. All three of the bunny egg cozies shown here are knitted from the same pattern, but with the simplest of embroidery their expressions range from puzzled to proud. In an assortment of colors, making these small projects is a great way to use up small amounts of leftover yarn. Alternatively, you can make three the same from one single 50g ball.

SIZE
To cover a large- to extra-large-sized egg

MATERIALS
Debbie Bliss Rialto DK (100% extra-fine merino wool, approx 115 yd per 1¾oz/50g ball)
One ball in main shade
Small amount of chocolate brown for embroidery
Pair of size 3 knitting needles

GAUGE
24 sts and 40 rows to 4in square over St st using size 3 needles.

ABBREVIATIONS
See page 10.

NOTES
Please note the egg cozy is worked with smaller than usually recommended needles for this yarn and the given gauge reflects this.

TO MAKE
With size 3 needles, cast on 36 sts.
Beg with a k row, work 18 rows in St st.
Dec row [K2tog] to end. *18 sts.*
P 1 row.
Dec row [K2tog] to end. *9 sts.*
Cut off yarn leaving a long yarn tail, thread through rem sts, pull to gather, and secure. Sew seam, reversing at lower edge to allow for roll.

EARS (MAKE 2)
With size 3 needles, cast on 12 sts.
K 30 rows.
Dec row Skp, k to last 2 sts, k2tog. *10 sts.*
K 1 row.
Rep the last 2 rows 4 times more. *2 sts.*
Next row K2tog and fasten off.
On cast-on edge, place a marker on 8th st for first ear and 4th st for second ear.
Fold cast-on edge of each ear, matching edge of row to marked st, secure, and then sew to head.
With chocolate brown yarn, embroider eyes and nose as shown.

29

Bead necklace

This necklace is a pretty addition to any jewelry collection. In order to make it, all that is required is the ability to knit garter stitch—the simplest stitch of all—small amounts of leftover yarn, some wooden beads, and a length of ribbon. I have used tonal pastel shades, but you could use stonger, more gemlike colors, or alternate uncovered beads with those covered with knitting.

SIZE
Approximately 60in long

MATERIALS
Debbie Bliss Eco Baby (100% organic cotton, approx 137 yd per 1¾oz/50g ball)
Small amount of in each of rose, pale pink, mauve, and lilac
Pair of size 2 knitting needles
Approximately 60in of satin ribbon, ⅛in wide
Nine wooden beads, 1in in diameter
Darning needle

GAUGE
25 sts and 34 rows to 4in square over St st using size 3 needles.

ABBREVIATIONS
See page 10.

TIP
The covers fit snugly over the beads when worked on size 2 needles in garter stitch and stretched to its full extent. However, the gauge given above is the recommended standard gauge for this yarn, not the gauge used.

TO MAKE
Make 3 in pale pink and 2 in each of rose, mauve, and lilac, making each one as follows:
With size 2 needles, cast on 2 sts.
1st row [Kfb] into each st.
2nd row K to end.
Rep these 2 rows 3 times more. *32 sts.*
K 4 rows.
Next row [K2tog] to end.
Next row K to end.
Rep the last 2 rows 3 times more. *2 sts.*
Next row K2tog and fasten off.

TO FINISH
With a darning needle thread the ribbon through the beads. Place a knitted piece over each bead, in a repeating sequence of pale pink, mauve, lilac, rose, ending with pale pink, then sew the side seam. Tie the ribbon to make the necklace, adjusting the length to suit.

a striking string of colorful beads

Bookmarks

An indispensible item for readers. It can be difficult to find something original to make to use up your leftover yarn, but these bookmarks fit the bill. You can work as many vertical lines as you like to create the woven effect so each one you make will look different. Use the delicate shades pictured here or brighter hues for a more vivid effect.

SIZE

Approximately 8in long, excluding the tied yarn ends

MATERIALS

Debbie Bliss Baby Cashmerino (55% merino wool, 33% microfiber, 12% cashmere, approx 137 yd per 1¾oz/50g ball)
Small amount in each of silver (A), pale pink (B), and white (C)
Pair of size 3 knitting needles
Large-eyed blunt-ended yarn needle

GAUGE

25 sts and 34 rows to 4in square over St st using size 3 needles.

ABBREVIATIONS

See page 10.

TO MAKE

With size 3 needles and A, cast on 3 sts, leaving a long end.
K 1 row.
P 1 row.
Next row (wrong side) K1, M1, k1, M1, k1. *5 sts.*
P 1 row
Next row K1, M1, k to last st, M1, k1. *7 sts.*
Rep the last 2 rows twice more. *11 sts.* **
Work even in St st until piece measures approximately 6¾in from **, ending with a p row.
Next row K1, ssk, k to last 3 sts, k2tog, k1.
P 1 row.
Rep the last 2 rows until 5 sts rem, ending with a p row.
Next row K1, sl 2tog, k1, pass 2 slipped sts over, k1. *3 sts.*
P 1 row.
Next row K3tog and fasten off, leaving a long end.

TO FINISH

Working from the right side (the p side), with lengths of B or C in the large-eyed needle, weave vertical lines into the stitches, leaving long ends at top and bottom. When all the lines have been woven in, knot the yarn ends into groups and trim. Press lightly.

Bow belt

The simplest garter stitch strip is embellished with spotty ribbon and a knitted bow to create this adorable belt. The ribbon ties at the back, making the belt fully adjustable, while contrasting strips of garter stitch make a bow at the front. If you prefer a simpler look, omit the knitted bow or tie the ribbon at the front.

SIZE
To tie around the waist

MATERIALS
Debbie Bliss Eco Baby (100% organic cotton, approx 137 yd per 1¾oz/50g ball)
One ball in silver gray (A) and a small amount in white (B)
Pair of size 2 knitting needles
2¼yd of grosgrain ribbon, ½in wide

GAUGE
28 sts and 49 rows to 4in square over garter st using size 2 needles.

ABBREVIATIONS
See page 10.

TIP
The length of the belt strip can be adjusted, if required, by knitting more or fewer rows, but as the ribbon extends beyond the length of the belt, this is not necessary.

BELT STRIP
With size 2 needles and A, cast on 10 sts and work in garter st (k every row) until strip measures 25½in.
Bind off.

BOW
With size 2 needles and B, cast on 14 sts and work in garter st for 8in.
Bind off.

CENTER STRIP
With size 2 needles and A, cast on 8 sts and work in garter st for 4in.
Bind off.

TO FINISH
Place a marker in the center of the belt strip. Fold the ribbon in half to find the center, then matching the ribbon foldline to the marker, sew the ribbon along the length in the center of the belt strip, leaving ribbon ends free. Sew together the cast-on and bound-off edges of the bow, and with the seam at the center back, sew to the center of the belt strip. Sew together the cast-on and bound-off edges of the narrow center strip, then slide this over the belt and the bow and sew to the back of the bow.

Sewing needle case

Knitted in duck egg blue cotton with chocolate brown and pale blue felt leaves, this sewing needle case is made using my all-time favorite color combination. Lined with a striped cotton fabric, this case will keep your sewing needles safely stored away.

SIZE
Approximately 4¼in x 3½in, when folded

MATERIALS
Debbie Bliss Eco Baby (100% organic cotton, approx 137 yd per 1¾oz/50g ball)
One ball in duck egg
Pair of size 2 knitting needles
7in x 4¾in of fine cotton fabric for lining
Two pieces of 6¼in x 4in felt

GAUGE
26 sts and 40 rows to 4in square over patt using size 2 needles.

ABBREVIATIONS
See page 10.

COVER
With size 2 needles, cast on 29 sts.
1st row (right side) K1, [p1, k1] to end.
2nd row P.
3rd row P1, [k1, p1] to end.
4th row P.
These 4 rows **form** the patt and are repeated.
Patt 32 rows more, so ending with a 4th patt row.
Foldline row (right side) P.
Next row P.
Beg with a 3rd row, work 37 rows in patt, so ending with a 3rd patt row.
Bind off knitwise.

TO FINISH
Fold ½in onto wrong side all around edge of lining fabric and press in place, folding in corners. Position lining centrally on wrong side of cover and slipstitch in place. Fold the two felt pieces in half and stitch together along the foldline, like pages in a book. Sew the felt pages to the center of the lined cover.

Baby cardigan

This pretty pastel top is knitted in seed stitch, a reversible fabric that still looks great when the sleeve cuffs and collars are turned back. It is worked in my Eco Baby yarn, an organic cotton produced under the Fairtrade banner, that is kind to baby, the environment, and the people who make it.

SIZES

To fit ages (in months)

3–6	6–9	9–12	

Finished measurements

Chest

18	20½	23½	in

Length to shoulder

10¼	11	12	in

Sleeve length

4¾	5½	6¼	in

MATERIALS

Debbie Bliss Eco Baby (100% organic cotton, approx 137 yd per 1¾oz/50g ball)
3 (4: 4) balls in pale pink
Pair each of sizes 2 and 3 knitting needles
27½in of narrow ribbon

GAUGE

25 sts and 42 rows to 4in square over seed st using size 3 needles.

ABBREVIATIONS

See page 10.

BACK

With size 3 needles, cast on 71 (81: 91) sts.
Seed st row K1, [p1, k1] to end. This row **forms** seed st and is repeated.
Cont in seed st until back measures 5½ (6: 6¼)in from cast-on edge, ending with a wrong-side row.

Dec row K1, [p3tog, yo, k1, p1, sl 1, k2tog, psso, yo, p1, k1] to end. *57 (65: 73) sts.*
Cont in seed st until back measures 6¼ (6¾: 7)in from cast-on edge, ending with a wrong-side row.
Shape sleeves
Cast on 38 (45: 52) sts at beg of next 2 rows. *133 (155: 177) sts.*
Work even until back measures 10¼ (11: 12)in from cast-on edge, ending with a wrong-side row.
Next row Seed st 47 (57: 67), bind off next 39 (41: 43) sts for back neck, seed st to end.
Leave these 2 sets of 47 (57: 67) sts on holders.

LEFT FRONT

With size 3 needles, cast on 35 (41: 47) sts.
Work in seed st until front measures 5½ (6: 6¼)in from cast-on edge, ending with a wrong-side row.
1st size only
Dec row K1, p1, k1, [p3tog, yo, k1, p1, sl 1, k2tog, psso, yo, p1, k1] to last 2 sts, p1, k1. *29 sts.*
2nd size only
Dec row K1, [p3tog, yo, k1, p1, sl 1, k2tog, psso, yo, p1, k1] to end. *33 sts.*
3rd size only
Dec row K1, [p1, k1] twice, [p3tog, yo, k1, p1, sl 1, k2tog, psso, yo, p1, k1] to last 2 sts, p1, k1. *39 sts.*
All sizes
Cont in seed st until front measures 6¼ (6¾: 7)in from cast-on edge, ending with a wrong-side row.
Shape sleeve
Cast on 38 (45: 52) sts at beg of next row. *67 (78: 91) sts.*
Work even until front measures 10¼ (11: 12)in from cast-on edge, ending with a wrong-side row.
Next row Seed st 47 (57: 67), bind off last 20 (21: 24) sts.
Leave rem sts on a holder.

RIGHT FRONT

With size 3 needles, cast on 35 (41: 47) sts.
Work in seed st until front measures 5½ (6: 6¼)in from cast-on edge, ending with a wrong-side row.
1st size only
Dec row K1, p1, k1, [p3tog, yo, k1, p1, sl 1, k2tog, psso, yo, p1, k1] to last 2 sts, p1, k1. *29 sts.*
2nd size only
Dec row K1 [p3tog, yo, k1, p1, sl 1, k2tog, psso, yo, p1, k1] to end. *33 sts.*
3rd size only
Dec row K1, [p1, k1] twice, [p3tog, yo, k1, p1, sl 1, k2tog, psso, yo, p1, k1] to last 2 sts, p1, k1. *39 sts.*
All sizes
Cont in seed st until front measures 6¼ (6¾: 7)in from cast-on edge, ending with a right-side row.
Shape sleeve
Cast on 38 (45: 52) sts at beg of next row. *67 (78: 91) sts.*
Work even until front measures 10¼ (11: 12)in from cast-on edge, ending with a wrong-side row.
Next row Bind off 20 (21: 24) sts, seed st to end.
Leave rem sts on a holder.

TO FINISH

Left shoulder Place sts on two needles with points facing the cuff edge. With right sides together and wrong sides facing, knitting one st from each needle together, bind off 14 (18: 22) sts, with one st on right-hand needle, then turn knitting so wrong sides are together and bind off rem sts.
Right shoulder Work to match left shoulder.
Sew side and underarm seams, reversing seam on last 2¼ (2¾: 3¼)in for cuff.
Thread ribbon through eyelets to tie at front.

freshen up shelves for springtime

Lace shelf edging

A pretty decorative edging adds some vintage style to an otherwise plain kitchen shelf. Knitted in a fine organic pure cotton, which gives great stitch detail, the lace pattern is worked over just 13 stitches and 12 rows so it and can be easily repeated until the edging is the length you require.

SIZE
Approximately 2½in at widest point

MATERIALS
Debbie Bliss Eco Baby (100% organic cotton, approx 137 yd per 1¾oz/50g ball)
One ball in white
Pair of size 3 knitting needles

GAUGE
25 sts and 34 rows to 4in square over St st using size 3 needles.

ABBREVIATIONS
yo2 yarn over twice (yarn around right-hand needle twice to make 2 new sts).
Also see page 10.

NOTE
One 50g ball of Eco Baby will make an edging approximately 57in long.

TO MAKE
With size 3 needles, cast on 13 sts.
1st row (right side) K2, k2tog, yo2, k2tog, k7.
2nd row K9, p1, k3.
3rd and 4th rows Knit.
5th row K2, k2tog, yo2, k2tog, k2, [yo2, k1] 3 times, yo2, k2. *21 sts.*
6th row K3, [p1, k2] 3 times, p1, k4, p1, k3.
7th and 8th rows Knit.
9th row K2, k2tog, yo2, k2tog, k15.
10th row K12 wrapping yarn twice around needle for each st, yo2, k5, p1, k3.
11th row K10, [p1, k1] into next st, slip next 12 sts onto right-hand needle, dropping extra loops, return sts to left-hand needle then k12tog. *13 sts.*
12th row Knit.
These 12 rows **form** the patt and are repeated until the edging is the length required, ending with an 11th patt row.
Bind off knitwise.

Gardener's gloves

Worked in fine cotton yarn, with a contrasting shade tipping the cuff and each finger and thumb end, these gloves are the perfect gift for any avid gardener. Because they are fingerless, they allow you to work on the more tricky tasks, such as pruning or tying up, but they are also pretty enough to wear outside of the garden, too.

SIZES
To fit small/medium (medium/large) hands

MATERIALS
Debbie Bliss Eco Baby (100% organic cotton, approx 137 yd per 1¾oz/50g ball)
One ball in apple (A) and a small amount in sage (B)
Pair each of sizes 2 and 3 knitting needles

GAUGE
25 sts and 30 rows to 4in square over St st using size 3 needles.

ABBREVIATIONS
See page 10.

RIGHT GLOVE
** With size 2 needles and B, cast 42 (50) sts.
1st rib row (right side) K2, [p2, k2] to end.
Change to A.
2nd rib row P2, [k2, p2] to end.
These 2 rows **form** the rib and are repeated using A only.
Rib 17 rows more.
Next row (wrong side) Rib to end and inc 8 sts evenly across row. *50 (58) sts.*
Change to size 3 needles.
Beg with a k row, work in St st throughout.
Work 8 rows **.
Shape thumb
Next row (right side) K25 (29), M1, k3, M1, k to end.
Work 3 rows.
Next row K25 (29), M1, k5, M1, k to end.
Work 1 row.
Next row K25 (29), M1, k7, M1, k to end.

Work 1 row.
Next row K25 (29), M1, k9, M1, k to end.
Work 1 row.
Cont to inc as set on 3 (4) foll right-side rows, working 2 sts more between each inc, ending with a p row. *64 (74) sts.*
Divide for thumb
Next row (right side) K42 (48), turn.
Next row P17 (19), turn.
Work 6 rows in St st on these 17 (19) sts only.
Change to B.
Work 2 rows.
Bind off.
Sew thumb seam.
With right side facing, join A to base of thumb, k to end. *47 (55) sts.*
Work 13 (15) rows in St st.
*** Divide for fingers
First (index) finger
Next row K30 (35), turn and cast on 2 sts.

Next row P15 (17), turn.

Work 6 rows in St st.

Change to B.

Work 2 rows.

Bind off.

Sew seam.

Second (middle) finger

With right side facing, join A to base of first finger, pick up and k 2 sts from cast-on sts at base of first finger, k6 (7), turn, cast on 2 sts.

Next row P16 (18), turn.

Work 8 rows in St st.

Change to B.

Work 2 rows.

Bind off.

Sew seam.

Third (ring) finger

With right side facing, join A to base of second finger, pick up and k 2 sts from cast-on sts at base of second finger, k6 (7), turn, cast on 2 sts.

Next row P16 (18), turn.

Work 6 rows in St st.

Change to B.

Work 2 rows.

Bind off.

Sew seam.

Fourth (little) finger

With right side facing, join A to base of third finger, pick up and k 2 sts from cast-on sts at base of third finger, k5 (6), turn.

Next row P12 (14).

Work 4 rows in St st.

Change to B.

Work 2 rows.

Bind off.

Sew seam.

LEFT GLOVE

Work as given for Right Glove from ** to **.

Shape thumb

Next row K22 (26), M1, k3, M1, k to end.

Work 3 rows.

Next row K22 (26), M1, k5, M1, k to end.

Work 1 row.

Next row K22 (26), M1, k7, M1, k to end.

Work 1 row.

Next row K22 (26), M1, k9, M1, k to end.

Work 1 row.

Cont to inc as set on every alt row until there are 64 (74) sts on needle.

Work 1 row.

Divide for thumb

Next row K39 (45), turn.

Next row P17 (19).

Work 6 rows in St st.

Change to B.

Work 2 rows.

Bind off.

Sew seam.

With right side facing, join A to base of thumb, k to end. *47 (55) sts.*

Work 13 (15) rows.

Complete as for Right Glove from *** to end.

Summer

Clothespin bag
To give your summer clothesline a touch of style, knit this simple clothespin bag. It is worked in a crisp textured stitch pattern in an aran-weight cotton yarn, which knits up quickly and easily. The striped-fabric lining adds a bright pop of color.

SIZE
Approximately 12¼in x 9¾in

MATERIALS
Debbie Bliss Eco Aran (100% organic cotton, approx 99 yd per 1¾oz/50g ball)
Three balls in duck egg
Pair of size 7 knitting needles
15in x 28in piece of fabric for lining
12in straight wooden clothes hanger

GAUGE
20 sts and 30 rows to 4in square over patt using size 7 needles.

ABBREVIATIONS
See page 10.

TIP
You may find it difficult to obtain a 12in wooden hanger, but you can cut a standard-width hanger to size using a small saw.

UPPER FRONT AND BACK
With size 7 needles, cast on 63 sts.
Next 2 rows K1, p1, turn, sl 1, p1.
Next 2 rows [K1, p1] twice, turn, sl 1, p3.
Next 2 rows [K1, p1] 3 times, turn, sl 1, p5.
Next 2 rows [K1, p1] 5 times, turn, sl 1, p9.
Next 2 rows [K1, p1] 7 times, turn, sl 1, p13.
Next 2 rows [K1, p1] 10 times, turn, sl 1, p19.
Next 2 rows [K1, p1] 13 times, turn, sl 1, p25.
Next row (right side) K1, [p1, k1] 31 times.
Next 2 rows P2, turn, sl 1, k1.
Next 2 rows P4, turn, sl 1, k1, p1, k1.
Next 2 rows P6, turn, sl 1, k1, [p1, k1] twice.
Next 2 rows P10, turn, sl 1, k1, [p1, k1] 4 times.
Next 2 rows P14, turn, sl 1, k1, [p1, k1] 6 times.
Next 2 rows P20, turn, sl 1, k1, [p1, k1] 9 times.
Next 2 rows P26, turn, sl 1, k1, [p1, k1] 13 times.
Next row P63.
Next row K1, [p1, k1] 31 times.
The last 2 rows **form** the pattern and are repeated.
Work even in patt until upper front measures 4in from cast-on edge, measured along the side edge and place a marker at each end of last row for top fold and mark the center st of this row.
Work even in patt for 10in more for bag back,

ending with a right-side row.
Bind off knitwise.

LOWER FRONT
With size 7 needles, cast on 63 sts.
Next 2 rows K1, p1, turn, sl 1, p1.
Next 2 rows [K1, p1] twice, turn, sl 1, p3.
Next 2 rows [K1, p1] 3 times, turn, sl 1, p5.
Next 2 rows [K1, p1] 4 times, turn, sl 1, p7.
Next 2 rows [K1, p1] 5 times, turn, sl 1, p9.
Next 2 rows [K1, p1] 6 times, turn, sl 1, p11.
Next 2 rows [K1, p1] 7 times, turn, sl 1, p13.
Next 2 rows [K1, p1] 8 times, turn, sl 1, p15.
Next 2 rows [K1, p1] 10 times, turn, sl 1, p19.
Next 2 rows [K1, p1] 12 times, turn, sl 1, p23.
Next 2 rows [K1, p1] 14 times, turn, sl 1, p27.
Next row (right side) K1, [p1, k1] 31 times.
Next 2 rows P2, turn, sl 1, k1.
Next 2 rows P4, turn, sl 1, k1, p1, k1.
Next 2 rows P6, turn, sl 1, k1, [p1, k1] twice.
Next 2 rows P8, turn, sl 1, k1, [p1, k1] 3 times.
Next 2 rows P10, turn, sl 1, k1, [p1, k1] 4 times.
Next 2 rows P12, turn, sl 1, k1, [p1, k1] 5 times.
Next 2 rows P14, turn, sl 1, k1, [p1, k1] 6 times.
Next 2 rows P16, turn, sl 1, k1, [p1, k1] 7 times.
Next 2 rows P20, turn, sl 1, k1, [p1, k1] 9 times.
Next 2 rows P24, turn, sl 1, k1, [p1, k1] 11 times.

keep your clothespins in line

Next 2 rows P28, turn, sl 1, k1, [p1, k1] 13 times.
Next row P63.
Next row K1, [p1, k1] 31 times.
The last 2 rows **form** the pattern and are repeated.
Work even in patt until lower front measures 10in from cast-on edge, measured along the side edge, ending with a right-side row.
Bind off knitwise.

LINING

Sew the bound-off edges of the two pieces together. Lay the knitted piece on the lining fabric and draw around the edge (for the stitching line) adding a ⅝in seam allowance around all edges. On the fabric, mark the position of the three upper-front yarn markers. Fold the fabric matching the side yarn markers of the upper front to the stitching line points at the top of the lower front and sew the seams, from the markers to the fold. Make ½in snips into the curved edges of the lining, fold, and press the seam allowances onto the wrong side.

TO FINISH

Matching the edges of the cast-on row of the lower front to the side-edge yarn markers of the upper front, sew the side seams of the knitted bag. Insert the lining into the bag and slipstitch the lining in place around the top edges. Make a small hole in the lining to accommodate the hook of the hanger. Insert the hanger hook through the small hole and the center marked stitch of the upper front, fold the upper front over onto the lower front, and stitch the sides, so forming the "envelope."

Chair cushion

Give your chair a 1950s-style "Doris Day" makeover with a gingham cushion that is far easier to knit than it looks. The back is worked in plain stockinette stitch while the check pattern uses the stranding technique. For a bolder alternative colorway, I would recommend using a hot pink.

SIZE
Approximately 13in square

MATERIALS
Debbie Bliss Rialto Aran (100% extra-fine merino wool, approx 88 yd per 1¾oz/50g ball)
Three balls in teal (A) and one ball in each of duck egg (B) and ecru (C)
Pair of size 7 knitting needles
1yd of cotton tape, ⅜in wide
13in square of foam sheet, ¾in thick

GAUGE
20 sts and 28 rows to 4in square over St st using size 7 needles.

ABBREVIATIONS
See page 10.

COVER
Back
With size 7 needles and A, cast on 67 sts.
Beg with a k row, work 97 rows in St st, so ending with a k row.
Foldline row (wrong side) K.
Front
Now work in St st in color patt as follows:
1st, 3rd, and 5th rows (right side) K6A, [k5B, k5A] to last st, k1A.
2nd, 4th, and 6th rows P6A, [p5B, p5A] to last st, p1A.
7th, 9th, and 11th rows K6B, [k5C, p5B] to last st, k1B.
8th, 10th, and 12th rows P6B, [p5C, p5B] to last st, p1B.
These 12 rows **form** the St st color patt and are

repeated 6 times more, then the first 6 rows again, so ending with a wrong-side row.
P 1 row in A.
Bind off knitwise in A.

TO FINISH
Fold in half along foldline row and sew side seams, leaving other side open. Cut the tape in two equal lengths, fold each length in half, and sew the fold to the wrong side of the open edge of the cushion back. Insert the foam pad and sew the open edges together.

String bag

The humble string bag has been transformed into this super stylish accessory. I have given it a "seaside" feel by knitting it in a bright white cotton yarn and edging it with nautical navy fabric binding.

SIZE
Approximately 22in from base to top of strap when empty

MATERIALS
Debbie Bliss Cotton DK (100% cotton, approx 92 yd per 1¾oz/50g ball)
Three balls in white
Pair each of sizes 7 and 13 knitting needles
2¼yd of bias binding, 1in wide

GAUGE
There is no need to measure the gauge as it is not important.

ABBREVIATIONS
See page 10.

TO MAKE
With size 7 needles, cast on 7 sts.
K 1 row
Next row [Kfb] 6 times, k1. *13 sts.*
K 1 row.
Next row K1, [kfb, k1] to end. *19 sts.*
K 1 row.
Next row [Kfb] to last st, k1. *37 sts.*
K 1 row.
Next row [K1, kfb] to last st, k1. *55 sts.*
K 1 row.
Next row K1, [kfb, k2] to end. *73 sts.*
K 1 row.
Change to size 13 needles.
K 47 rows.
Next row K36, k2tog, k to end.
Divide for strap
Change to size 7 needles.
Next row K2tog, k32, k2tog, turn and cont on these 34 sts, leave rem 36 sts on a holder.
** K 1 row.
Next row K2tog, k to last 2 sts, k2tog.
Rep the last 2 rows until 10 sts rem.
K 60 rows.
Bind off. **
With correct side facing, rejoin yarn to first st on holder, k2tog, k to last 2 sts, k2tog.
Rep as first side of strap from ** to **.

TO FINISH
Sew bound-off edges of strap together. Sew together row-end edges of bag from strap divide to cast-on edge, then thread the yarn along cast-on edge, pull to gather, and secure. Fold the binding over all the row-end edges and stitch in place, folding under binding ends.

Baby sandals

As a change from the traditional baby socks or booties, why not try a summery version with this take on the classic sandal? Worked in garter stitch and stockinette stitch to create a firm fabric, the ankle strap slots through a loop at the front and then fastens with a button at the side.

SIZE
To fit ages 3–12 months

MATERIALS
Debbie Bliss Eco Baby (100% organic cotton, approx 137 yd per 1¾oz/50g ball)
One ball in navy
Pair of size 2 knitting needles
2 buttons

GAUGE
25 sts and 34 rows to 4in square over St st on size 3 needles.

ABBREVIATIONS
See page 10.

NOTE
The sandals are worked in garter stitch on smaller than usually recommended needles. The gauge given is the standard for this yarn in stockinette stitch, so check your gauge in stockinette stitch.

RIGHT SANDAL
With size 2 needles, cast on 36 sts and k one row.
1st row (right side) K1, yo, k16, yo, [k1, yo] twice, k16, yo, k1.
2nd and all wrong-side rows K to end, working tbl into each yo of previous row.
3rd row K2, yo, k16, yo, k2, yo, k3, yo, k16, yo, k2.
5th row K3, yo, k16, yo, [k4, yo] twice, k16, yo, k3.
7th row K4, yo, k16, yo, k5, yo, k6, yo, k16, yo, k4.
9th row K5, yo, k16, yo, [k7, yo] twice, k16, yo, k5.
11th row K22, yo, k8, yo, k9, yo, k22. *64 sts.*
Shape instep
Next row K36, skp, turn.
Next row Sl 1, p8, p2tog, turn.
Next row Sl 1, k8, skp, turn.
Rep the last 2 rows 7 times more, then work first of the 2 rows again.
Next row Sl 1, k to end.
Next row K17, k2tog, p8, skp, k17. *44 sts.*
Next row K24, turn.
Next row P4, turn.
Next row K4, turn.
Work 2¼in in St st on these 4 sts only for front strap.
Bind off.

With right side facing, rejoin yarn at base of strap, pick up and k 12 sts along side edge of strap. Turn and bind off knitwise all sts at this side of strap.
With right side facing, rejoin yarn to top of other side of strap, pick up and k 12 sts along side edge of strap, then k rem 20 sts.
Bind off knitwise.
Sew sole and back heel seam.
Place markers on 9th st at each side of back seam.
With right side facing and size 2 needles, pick up and k 18 sts between markers along heel edge for ankle strap. **
Next row Cast on 22, k to end, turn and cast on 4 sts. *44 sts.*
Buttonhole row K to last 3 sts, k2tog, yo, k1.
K 2 rows.
Bind off.
Fold front strap over ankle strap to wrong side and slipstitch bound-off edge in place. Sew on button.

LEFT SANDAL
Work as given for Right Sandal to **.
Next row Cast on 4 sts, k to end, turn and cast on 22 sts. *44 sts.*
Buttonhole row K1, yo, skp, k to end.
Complete as Right Sandal.

precious yet practical
baby sandals

Pencil case

One of the pleasures of going back to school—or perhaps the only one—is the prospect of brand new pens, pencils, and other stationery for the new school year. Send them back to class with their pencils packed away in this smart tartan zip-up case with a contrasting fabric lining. Knit this pencil case over summer vacation ready for the start of school in the fall.

SIZE
Approximately 3½in x 9in

MATERIALS
Debbie Bliss Rialto DK (100% extra-fine merino wool, approx 115 yd per 1¾oz/50g ball)
One ball in each of teal (A) and mint green (B)
Pair of size 6 knitting needles
8¼in x 10¼in piece of cotton lining fabric
8in zipper
Sewing thread and needle

GAUGE
22 sts and 30 rows to 4in square over St st using size 6 needles.

ABBREVIATIONS
See page 10.

TO MAKE
With size 6 needles and A, cast on 61 sts.
K 1 row.
Beg with a k row, work 22 rows in St st from chart 1 (see page 61), so ending with a p row.
K 3 rows in A only.
Beg with a p row, work 22 rows in St st from chart 2, so ending with a k row.
P 2 rows in A.
Bind off knitwise in A on wrong-side row.

head back to
school in style

CHART 1

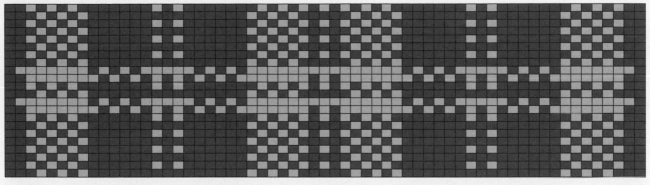

CHART 2

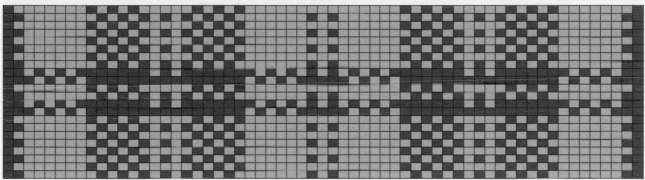

KEY
A teal
B mint green

TO FINISH

Fold knitting in half lengthwise along central foldline and sew side edges together, working mattress stitch through the center of the edge stitch and leaving cast-on and bound-off edges open. Sew cast-on to bound-off edge, for approximately ½in at each end. Pin, baste, and hand stitch zipper in place.

Fold lining fabric in half lengthwise and taking ⅝in seams, sew side seams, from fold to raw edges, then continue to sew top seam for approximately ½in at each end. Press ⅝in onto wrong side along open edges. Insert lining into pencil case and hand stitch lining to zipper tape.

To assist opening and closing, cut a few lengths of yarn, thread through zipper pull, and tie in a knot.

Lacy scarf

What could be simpler than this four-row lace pattern knitted in a crisp organic cotton to create the perfect summer scarf? The lovely openwork effect makes it light and delicate , while the two-color stripes of taupe and white add a touch of sophistication. The cast-on edge of the stitch pattern forms a decorative scalloped edge so the scarf is worked in two halves and joined in the middle to give this effect at both ends.

SIZE
Approximately 5in x 63in (measured along side edge)

MATERIALS
Debbie Bliss Eco Baby (100% organic cotton, approx 137 yd per 1¾oz/50g ball)
Two balls in each of stone (A) and white (B)
Pair of size 3 knitting needles

GAUGES
25 sts and 34 rows over St st and 29 sts and 32 rows over patt, both to 4in square using size 3 needles.

ABBREVIATIONS
See page 10.

SCARF (MAKE 2)
With size 3 needles and A, cast on 38 sts.
Working in stripes of 4 rows A and 4 rows B, work in patt as follows:
1st row (right side) Knit.
2nd row Purl.
3rd row K1, * [k2tog] 3 times, [yo, k1] 6 times, [k2tog] 3 times; rep from * once more, k1.
4th row Knit.
Cont in 4 row stripes until scarf measures approximately 30¾in from cast-on edge, ending with a 2nd row in A for one piece and 1st row in A for second piece.
Leave sts on a spare needle.

TO FINISH
With wrong sides together, hold the 2 needles side by side and with a 3rd needle work: k2tog (by taking one st from each needle and working them together each time), k2tog and pass first st over second st and off the needle, bind off all sts in this way, so joining the two pieces together.

Votive candle-holder covers

Pure white cotton covers slipped over glass tumblers eminate the softest diffuse candlelight when filled with lit votive candles. These knitted lacy bands are relatively straightforward to make, take just 7 grams of yarn each, and really are a precious yet inexpensive gift.

SIZE

To fit a 2¾in diameter straight-sided glass tumbler

MATERIALS

Debbie Bliss Rialto 4-ply (100% extra-fine merino wool, approx 110 yd per 1¾oz/50g ball)
One ball in white
Pair of size 3 knitting needles

GAUGE

28 sts and 38 rows to 4in square over St st using size 3 needles.

ABBREVIATIONS

See page 10.

NOTE

Small amounts of leftover yarn can be used for the covers, as each cover weighs only approximately 7 grams.

TO MAKE

With size 3 needles, cast on 19 sts.
1st row (right side) K18, yo, k1.
2nd row Bind off 1 st, k to end.
3rd row K8, [k2tog, yo] 4 times, k2, yo, k1.
4th row Bind off 1 st, k next 3 sts, [yo, p2tog] 4 times, k7.
5th row K6, [k2tog, yo] 4 times, k4, yo, k1.
6th row Bind off 1 st, k next 5 sts, [yo, p2tog] 4 times, k5.
7th row K4, [k2tog, yo] 4 times, k6, yo, k1.
8th row Bind off 1 st, k next 7 sts, [yo, p2tog] 4 times, k3.
9th row K2, [k2tog, yo] 4 times, k8, yo, k1.
10th row Bind off 1 st, k next 9 sts, [yo, p2tog] 4 times, k1.
These 10 rows **form** the patt and are repeated 7 times more.
Bind off.

TO FINISH

Sew together cast-on and bound-off edges.
Slip cover over glass tumbler making sure the top edge of the knitted piece sits well below top edge of the glass.

SAFTEY NOTE

Never leave lit candles unattended and keep away from children.

65

Lavender bags
Perfume your drawers or wardrobes with these sweet-smelling lavender-filled pyramids, knitted in seed stitch. Using summery pastel shades from my lightweight Eco Baby yarn, the unusual shape gives a contemporary twist to the traditional lavender sachet.

SIZE
Approximately 3¼in high

MATERIALS
Debbie Bliss Eco Baby (100% organic cotton, approx 137 yd per 1¾oz/50g ball)
One ball in primrose, mauve, or duck egg
Pair of size 2 knitting needles
Approximately 1 ounce of dried lavender flowers for each bag
6in of narrow ribbon (optional)

GAUGE
26 sts and 45 rows to 4in square over seed st using size 2 needles.

ABBREVIATIONS
See page 10.

TO MAKE
With size 2 needles, cast on 21 sts.
Seed st row K1, [p1, k1] to end.
Rep this row until piece measures 6¼in.
Bind off.

TO FINISH
Sew cast-on to bound-off edge to form a tube.
Flatten the tube at one end, with the seam centrally placed and sew together the row-end edges.
Flatten the open end of the tube and with the seam to one side, sew together the row-end edges, leaving approximately 1½in of the seam open.
Fill with dried lavender flowers and sew the seam closed.
If you wish to hang the lavender bag, sew a loop of narrow ribbon to the top.

*sweetly scented
lavender sachets*

keep baby cool
in soft cotton

Striped baby hat

This simple hat is my idea of a really relaxing knit as it can be whipped up in next to no time. But why stop at just one? Baby could have a different color stripe combination for each day of the week. Made in cooling cotton, this hat takes little yarn and will protect baby's precious head from the sun's rays.

SIZE
To fit ages 6–12 months

MATERIALS
Debbie Bliss Eco Aran (100% organic cotton, approx 99 yd per 1¾oz/50g ball)
One ball in each of teal (A) and white (B)
Pair of size 8 knitting needles
Two size 8 double-pointed knitting needles

GAUGE
18 sts and 24 rows to 4in square over St st using size 8 needles.

ABBREVIATIONS
See page 10.

TO MAKE
With size 8 needles and A, cast on 65 sts.
Beg with a k row, work 28 rows in St st (in stripes of 4 rows A and 4 rows B alternately), so ending with a p row.
Cont in St st and work 2 rows in B.
Shape top
Next row With B, k1, [k2tog, k6] 8 times. *57 sts.*
P 1 row in B.
Next row With A, k1, [k2tog, k5] 8 times. *49 sts.*
P 1 row in A.
Next row With A, k1, [k2tog, k4] 8 times. *41 sts.*
P 1 row in A.
Next row With B, k1, [k2tog, k3] 8 times. *33 sts.*
P 1 row in B.
Next row With B, k1, [k2tog, k2] 8 times. *25 sts.*
P 1 row in B.
Next row With A, k1, [k2tog] 12 times. *13 sts.*
P 1 row in A.
Next row With A, k1, [k2tog] 6 times. *7 sts.*
Do not cut off yarn.

STALK
Slip rem 7 sts onto a size 8 double-pointed needle.
Cont in A only and with right side facing, place needle in left hand, pull yarn tightly from last st to first st across wrong side, and k7.
With right side still facing, slide these 7 sts to the opposite end of the same needle, place needle in left hand, pull yarn tightly from last st to first st across wrong side, and k7.
Rep the last row 4 times more.
Cut off yarn, leaving a long end, thread through sts, pull to gather, and secure.
Take yarn end down through stalk and sew together hat seam, matching stripes.

Striped pillow

Stockinette stitch stripes of taupe on a chalky white pillow cover will add a touch of elegance to a room. Work a single strip of knitting with simple buttonholes, sew up the side seams, add a few chunky buttons and... you're all done! As a variation on the theme, try white stripes on a taupe base.

SIZE
Approximately 14in wide x 15¼in tall

MATERIALS
Debbie Bliss Cotton DK (100% cotton, approx 92 yd per 1¾oz/50g ball)
Three balls in white (A) and two balls in stone (B)
Pair of size 6 knitting needles
14in square pillow form
4 buttons

GAUGE
20 sts and 28 rows to 4in square over St st using size
6 needles.

ABBREVIATIONS
See page 10.

NOTE
The pillow cover is made in one piece, working from the top edge of the back, down to the foldline, then up the front to the top edge. It is fastened at the top with four buttons.

TO MAKE
Cover back
With size 6 needles and A, cast on 70 sts.
Beg with a k row, work 9 rows in St st in A only, so ending with a k row.
Beg with a p row, cont to work in St st in stripe sequence as follows:
[2 rows in B, 2 rows in A] twice, 2 rows in B,
4 rows in A.
These 14 rows **form** the stripe patt and are repeated 6 times more, so ending with a k row.
Cover front
Foldline row (wrong side) With A, k to end.
Beg with a k row, cont in St st, working in stripe sequence as follows:
4 rows in A, [2 rows in B, 2 rows in A] twice,
2 rows in B.
These 14 rows **form** the stripe patt (a reverse of the cover back) and are repeated 6 times more, so ending with a p row.
Change to A and work 2 rows in St st.
Buttonhole row (right side) With A, k7, k2tog, yo, k16, k2tog, yo, k16, yo, k2tog, k16, yo, k2tog, k7.
Beg with a p row, work 6 rows more in St st in
A only, so ending with a k row.
Bind off knitwise.

TO FINISH
Fold cover in half along the foldline row and sew the side seams, matching the stripes. Sew buttons to the inside of the back to correspond with the buttonholes. Slip the pillow form into the cover and fasten the buttons.

Clothes hanger

This simple covered clothes hanger is the perfect starter project for a beginner knitter: work a straight strip of seed stitch in your chosen color, stretch it over a padded hanger, sew in place, then finish it off with a decorative ribbon bow. Worked in an aran-weight cotton yarn, this really is a quick knit.

SIZE
To fit an 18in plain wooden clothes hanger

MATERIALS
Debbie Bliss Eco Aran (100% organic cotton, approx 99 yd per 1¾oz/50g ball)
One ball in white
Pair of size 7 knitting needles
Batting
Plain wooden clothes hanger
20in of ribbon (optional)

GAUGE
19 sts and 30 rows to 4in square over seed st using size 7 needles.

ABBREVIATIONS
See page 10.

NOTE
Before beginning the cover, pad the hanger with batting and secure it in place with a few stitches.

COVER
With size 7 needles, cast on 69 sts.
Seed st row (right side) K1, [p1, k1] to end.
This row **forms** seed st and is repeated throughout.
Cont in seed st until work measures approximately 4¾in from cast-on edge.
Bind off in seed st.

TO FINISH
Fold the cover in half and sew together the row-end edges from fold to cast-on/bound-off edge. Find the center of the foldline and thread the hanger hook through the cover. Stretch the cover over the padded hanger and sew cast-on edge to bound-off edge.
Tie a length of tape or ribbon around the hook.

nautical but nice
summer holdall

Beach bag

The nautical look is always a favorite during the summer season. This rib and cable bag in knitted in the classic navy and white colorway, but its cheerful spot print lining gives it a modern edge. Whether you're on the deck of a cruise liner or heading to the beach, this bag is just right for carrying your vacation essentials.

SIZE

Approximately 15¾in x 12in x 3½in

MATERIALS

Debbie Bliss Eco Aran (100% organic cotton, approx 99 yd per 1¾oz/50g ball)
Six balls in navy (A) and one 50g ball in white (B)
Pair of size 7 knitting needles
Cable needle
2⅝yd of cotton tape, 1½in wide
55½in x 12in of very stiff interlining, such as buckram
34in of nonstretch cotton lining fabric, 36in wide

GAUGE

19 sts and 26 rows to 4in square over St st using size 7 needles.

ABBREVIATIONS

C6F slip next 3 sts onto cable needle and hold to front of work, k3, then k3 from cable needle.
Also see page 10.

NOTE

The bag is worked in one piece.

TO MAKE

Front

With size 7 needles and A, cast on 110 sts.

1st row (right side) K2, [p2, k2] to end.

2nd row P2, [k2, p2] to end.

** Change to B and k one row.

4th row Rep 2nd row.

5th row Rep 1st row.

6th row Rep 2nd row.

Change to A and k one row **.

8th row Rep 2nd row.

Rep from ** to ** once more.

*** Cont in A only in patt as follows:

1st row (wrong side) [P2, k2] 4 times, [p6, k2, p2, k2] 7 times, [p2, k2] twice, p2.

2nd row [K2, p2] 4 times, [k6, p2, k2, p2] 7 times, [k2, p2] twice, k2.

3rd row Rep 1st row.

4th row [K2, p2] 4 times, [C6F, p2, k2, p2] 7 times, [k2, p2] twice, k2.

5th–8th rows [Rep 1st and 2nd rows] twice.

These 8 rows **form** the rib and cable patt and are repeated.

Cont in patt until bag measures 10in from ***, ending with a wrong-side row.

Shape for base

Bind off 11 sts at beg of next 2 rows. *88 sts.*

Cont in patt as set until base measures 3½in, ending with a wrong-side row.

Back

Next row Cast on 11 sts and work [k2, p2] twice, k2, p1 across these sts, patt to end.

Next row Cast on 11 sts and work [p2, k2] twice, p2, k1 across these sts, patt to end. **** *110 sts.*

Cont in patt as set until bag back measures 10in from ****, ending with a wrong-side row.

Change to B and k 1 row.

Next row (wrong side) P2, [k2, p2] to end.

Next row K2, [p2, k2] to end.

Next row P2, [k2, p2] to end.

Change to A and k 1 row.

Next row P2, [k2, p2] to end.

Change to B and k 1 row.

Next row P2, [k2, p2] to end.

Next row K2, [p2, k2] to end.

Next row P2, [k2, p2] to end.

Change to A and k 1 row.

Next row P2, [k2, p2] to end.

Bind off in A, working p2tog across each pair of purl sts while binding off.

TO FINISH

Lay the piece, right side down, on a flat surface and starting at the base, pin the cotton tape in place, so that it runs behind the second cable from the right-hand edge, up the bag back, then leave approximately 20in free for back handle (this length is adjustable), continue to pin in place behind the second cable from the left-hand edge down the bag back, across the base and up the bag front following the same cable, then leave approximately 20in free for front handle, making sure it is the same length as the first handle, and continue to pin in place down to the base to meet up with the beginning of the tape. Stitch tape in place along both edges and across the tape at the top of the bag. Cut away any excess tape at the base, where it crosses. Sew side seams of bag from cast-on/bound-off edges down to base, then sew cast-on/bound-off edges of base shaping to row-ends of base with side seam placed centrally.

From interlining, cut two pieces 15¾in x 11in for sides, two pieces 3½in x 11in for ends and one piece 3½in x 15¾in for base. Turn bag inside out and hand sew interling to wrong side of bag.

LINING

From fabric, cut a piece 20½in x 29in. With right sides together, fold fabric in half across the width and taking ⅝in seam allowances, sew the side seams from fold to cut edges. Press seams open. Open out and refold the lining to form the bottom corners so that the side seams match the original fold, then stitch across the points so the seams are 3½in long to match the width of the bag base. Trim away the excess seam allowance at the corners. Press a ¾in hem onto the wrong side around the top edge. Insert lining into bag and slipstitch in place around the edge.

Flags

Create your very own "united nations" with these fun flags. As I live in the UK but spend a lot of time in the US, I feel an affinity with both the Union Jack and the Stars and Stripes. However, I have included the Greek flag, too, as a reminder of a wonderful recent vacation in Corfu. Each flag uses only scraps of the different yarn colors, plus one bamboo knitting needle to make an ideal flag pole.

SIZE
Approximately 6¼in x 4in

MATERIALS
Debbie Bliss Rialto 4-ply (100% extra-fine merino wool, approx 110 yd per 1¾oz/50g ball)
One ball in each color (or leftover yarns) as follows:
US red (A), white (B), and blue (C)
UK red (A), white (B), and blue (C)
Greece pale blue (A) and white (B)
Pair of size 3 knitting needles
Small amount of cotton fabric for backing
One size 8 bamboo knitting needle for each flag (for display)

GAUGE
28 sts and 38 rows to 4in square over St st using size 3 needles.

ABBREVIATIONS
See page 10.

NOTE
Each flag is worked from a chart using the relevant colors (see pages 80 and 81).

TO MAKE
With size 3 needles, cast on 47 sts for US and Greek flags and 46 sts for UK flag.
Beg with a k row, work in St st from the relevant chart (see pages 80 and 81) until all chart rows have been completed.
Bind off.

TO FINISH
US flag only
Following chart 1, work the stars in duplicate stitch on the flag.
All flags
Press lightly on the wrong side. Cut a piece of backing fabric slightly larger than the flag. With right sides together, lay the flag on the backing fabric and pin in place. Handstitch the backing to the flag around the two long sides and the short side without the selvage stitches. Trim away the excess fabric around the stitched edges. Turn right-side out and press. Fold the backing fabric to the inside along the open edge, leaving the selvage stitches free, then slipstitch the backing fabric in place along the fold. Fold the selvage stitches of the flag onto the back of the flag and slipstitch to the backing, leaving both ends open, so forming a channel for the flag pole. Insert the bamboo needle into the channel.

CHART 1 (US)

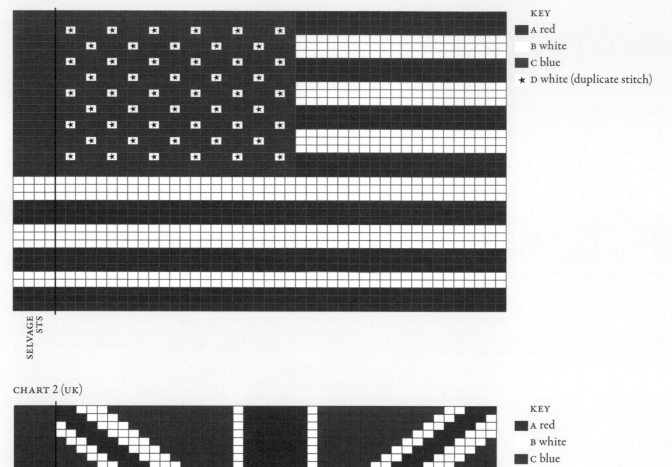

KEY

■ A red
□ B white
■ C blue
★ D white (duplicate stitch)

SELVAGE STS

CHART 2 (UK)

KEY

■ A red
□ B white
■ C blue

SELVAGE STS

CHART 3 (GREECE)

SELVAGE
ST5

Fall

Leftover yarns knitting bag

Every knitter needs a catchall for their yarns, needles, and work in progress. I can think of no better way of creating a knitting bag than to make it from your own stash. Working just two rows of garter stitch in each color creates fine stripes. I used a combination of eight different colors, but you could use more or fewer shades depending on what leftover yarns you have at hand.

SIZE
Approximately 14¼in wide at base and 12in tall

MATERIALS
Debbie Bliss Rialto Aran (100% extra-fine merino wool, approx 88 yd per 1¾oz/50g ball)
A total of approximately 200g in assorted colors (see YARN NOTES)
Pair of size 7 knitting needles
⅝yd of nonstretch cotton lining fabric
Sewing thread
Two 11in lengths of bamboo cane (approximately ½in in diameter)

GAUGE
20 sts and 44 rows to 4in square over garter st using size 7 needles.

ABBREVIATIONS
See page 10.

YARN NOTES
* I used one 50g ball of Debbie Bliss Rialto Aran in each of charcoal (A), cloud (B), toffee (C), gold (D), terracotta (E), light green (F), denim (G), and washed denim (H).
* If you use fewer colors or a single color, you may use less yarn than the total stated.

FRONT AND BACK (BOTH ALIKE)
With size 7 needles and A, cast on 73 sts.
K 1 row.
Now work in 2-row repeating garter st stripes of B, C, D, E, F, G, H, and A throughout, shaping as follows:
K 15 rows.
Dec row (wrong side) K14, k2tog tbl, k41, k2tog, k14. *71 sts.*
K 9 rows.
Dec row K14, k2tog tbl, k39, k2tog, k14. *69 sts.*
K 9 rows.
Dec row K14, k2tog tbl, k37, k2tog, k14. *67 sts.*
K 9 rows.
Cont in this way to dec 4 sts on every foll 10th row until 57 sts rem, ending with a dec row.
K 3 rows.
Shape for handles
Next row (wrong side) K20, bind off 17 sts, k to end and cont on this second set of 20 sts only, leave the first set of 20 sts on a holder.

K 1 row.
Next row (wrong side) K2, k2tog, k to end.
K 3 rows.
Rep the last 4 rows 5 times more, so ending with a right-side row.
Bind off rem 14 sts knitwise.
With right side facing, rejoin yarn to 20 sts on holder, k to end.
Next row (wrong side) K to last 4 sts, k2tog tbl, k2.
K 3 rows.
Rep the last 4 rows 5 times more, so ending with a right-side row.
Bind off rem 14 sts knitwise.

TO FINISH
Place markers on side edges, 8¼in up from cast-on edge. Using one knitted piece as a template, cut two pieces of lining fabric, adding ⅝in around all edges for seams and mark the position of the markers. Sew the knitted pieces together along cast-on edges and side edges up to markers. Sew fabric pieces together in the same way as the knitted pieces around the side and lower edges between the markers. Insert lining into bag and slipstitch around edges, leaving a gap at the top of the inner edge of the handle as shown. Insert bamboo canes for handles.

Cabled socks
Over-the-knee socks make a bold fashion statement, but they can also be worn rolled down—either way they keep toes cozy and are great for snuggling up in with a cup of hot chocolate and a favorite book. Knitted in my Baby Cashmerino yarn, the blend of merino wool, cashmere, and microfiber makes them soft to the touch but hardwearing.

SIZE
To fit women's shoe size 6–8

MATERIALS
Debbie Bliss Baby Cashmerino (55% merino wool, 33% microfiber, 12% cashmere, approx 137 yd per 1¾oz/50g ball)
Six balls in charcoal
Set of four size 3 double-pointed knitting needles
Cable needle

GAUGE
25 sts and 34 rows over St st and 32 sts and 34 rows over patt, both to 4in square using size 3 needles.

ABBREVIATIONS
C2B slip next st onto cable needle and hold at back of work, k1, then k1 from cable needle.
C2F slip next st onto cable needle and hold to front of work, k1, then k1 from cable needle.
Also see page 10.

TO MAKE
With size 3 needles, cast on 88 sts.
Arrange sts onto 3 of the 4 needles.
Work in rounds of twisted rib as follows:
1st round [K1tbl, p1] to end.
Rep the last round for 3¼in.
Inc row Rib 5, [M1, rib 8] to last 3 sts, M1, rib 3. *99 sts.*
Cont in patt as follows:
1st round [K1tbl, p2, k4, p2] to end.
2nd round Rep 1st round.
3rd round [K1tbl, p2, C2B, C2F, p2] to end.
4th round Rep 1st round.
These 4 rounds **form** the patt and are repeated.
Cont in patt until sock measures 13½in, ending with a 2nd round.
Dec round [K1tbl, p2tog, C2B, C2F, p2tog] to end. *77 sts.*
Cont in patt until sock measures 19in, ending with a 3rd round.
Dec round [K1tbl, p1, k2, skp, p1] to end. *66 sts.*
Cut off yarn.
Shape heel
Re-arrange sts as follows: slip next 13 sts onto first needle, next 20 sts onto second needle, next 21 sts onto third needle, and last 12 sts onto end of first needle.
Rejoin yarn to beg of first needle and work in rows as follows:
Next row (right side) K24, turn.

Next row Slip 1, p22, turn.
Next row Slip 1, k21, turn.
Next row Slip 1, p20, turn.
Cont in this way, working one less st on every row until the foll row has been worked:
Next row (wrong side) Slip 1, p10, turn.
Cont as follows:
Next row Slip 1, k11, turn.
Next row Slip 1, p12, turn.
Cont in this way, working one more st on every row until the foll row has been worked:
Next row Slip 1, p24, turn. **
With right side facing, slip next 25 sts onto first needle, next 20 sts onto second needle, and next 21 sts onto third needle and work in rounds as follows:
Next round (right side) K25, p1, [k1 tbl, p1] to end of round.
Rep the last round until sock measures 6¼in from **.
Next round K26, * [k2tog] twice, k1; rep from * to end. *50 sts.*

Shape toe
Next round [K1, skp, k19, k2tog, k1] twice.
Next round K to end.
Next round [K1, skp, k17, k2tog, k1] twice.
Next round K to end.
Next round [K1, skp, k15, k2tog, k1] twice.
Next round K to end.
Cont in rounds decreasing on every alt round as set until the foll round has been worked:
Next round [K1, skp, k7, k2tog, k1] twice.
22 sts.
Slip first 11 sts onto one needle and rem 11 sts onto a second needle.
Fold sock inside out and bind off one st from each needle together.

Potholder

If you are new to knitting and bored with endless practice samples, give yourself a sense of purpose by knitting up this practical potholder. Add a splash of color into your kitchen by knitting it in this shade of orange shown here. Whatever color you choose, line the knitted piece with insulation and fabric and add a loop.

SIZE
Approximately 6¾in x 7in

MATERIALS
Debbie Bliss Eco Aran (100% organic cotton, approx 99 yd per 1¾oz/50g ball)
One ball in orange
Pair of size 7 knitting needles
6¾in x 7in piece of batting or felt (for added insulation)
7¾in x 8in piece of cotton fabric (for backing)
5in piece of narrow ribbon

GAUGE
19½ sts and 26½ rows to 4in square over patt using size 7 needles.

ABBREVIATIONS
See page 10.

TO MAKE
With size 7 needles, cast on 33 sts.
1st and 10th rows K1, [p7, k1] to end.
2nd and 9th rows P1, [k7, p1] to end.
3rd and 12th rows K2, [p5, k3] to last 7 sts, p5, k2.
4th and 11th rows P2, [k5, p3] to last 7 sts, k5, p2.
5th and 14th rows K3, [p3, k5] to last 6 sts, p3, k3.
6th and 13th rows P3, [k3, p5] to last 6 sts, k3, p3.
7th and 16th rows K4, [p1, k7] to last 5 sts, p1, k4.
8th and 15th rows P4, [k1, p7] to last 5 sts, k1, p4.
These 16 rows **form** the pattern and are repeated twice more, binding off on the last 16th patt row.

TO FINISH
Overcast stitch batting or felt piece to back of knitted piece. Press ½in onto wrong side on all edges of fabric piece. Fold ribbon in half to form a loop, stitch ends together to hold in place, and pin to one corner of fabric piece. Slipstitch fabric to backed knitted piece.

Pompom handwarmers

Keep your hands cozy but your fingers free with these cute handwarmers. Given in two sizes, to fit either an adult or a child, these fingerless mittens are worked in chunky ribbing in Baby Cashmerino and incorporate a contrasting border. Perky pompoms dangling from simple crochet cords, tied in a bow, finish them off.

SIZE
To fit child's (adult's) hands

MATERIALS
Debbie Bliss Baby Cashmerino (55% merino wool, 33% micro-fiber, 12% cashmere, approx 137 yd per 1¾oz/50g ball)
One ball in each of mid brown (A) and rose pink (B)
Pair of 3.25 knitting needles
Size D-3 crochet hook
Large-eyed, blunt-ended yarn needle

GAUGE
25 sts and 34 rows to 4in square over St st using size 3 needles.

ABBREVIATIONS
See page 10.

TO MAKE (BOTH ALIKE)
With size 3 needles and A, cast on 42 (67) sts.
1st row (right side) P2, [k3, p2] to end.
2nd row K2 [p3, k2] to end.
These 2 rows **form** the rib pattern and are repeated throughout.
Work 38 (48) rows more in rib.
Shape thumb
Next row (right side) Rib 25 (38) sts, turn.
Next row Cast on 5 sts, rib 13 (14) sts, turn.
Cont on these 13 (14) sts only.
Rib 3 rows.
Change to B and rib 2 rows more.
Bind off in rib.
Sew thumb seam.
With right side facing, rejoin A at base of thumb and pick up and k 3 (4) sts from 5 cast-on sts, then rib to end. *37 (62) sts.*
Rib 12 rows.
Change to B and rib 2 rows more.
Bind off in rib.

TO FINISH
Sew side seam on each handwarmer.
With size D-3 crochet hook and B, make two lengths of chains each approximately 16in long. Starting and finishing at the side seam, about 1½in from cast-on edge, thread a chain through the ribs of each handwarmer, using a large-eyed, blunt-ended yarn needle.
With B, make four small pompoms and sew one to each end of each chain.

Cabled seed stitch beret

I have knitted this beret in a classic shade of dark gray for a little continental chic. However, if gray feels like too much of a school uniform color for your child, get them to choose an alternative hue. The cables are generously proportioned and provide textural contrast set against the seed stitch panels.

SIZE
To fit a 3–5 year-old child

MATERIALS
Debbie Bliss Rialto DK (100% extra-fine merino wool, approx 115 yd per 1¾oz/50g ball)
Two balls in charcoal
Pair of size 6 knitting needles
Two size 3 double-pointed knitting needles
Cable needle

GAUGE
22 sts and 40 rows to 4in square over seed st using size 6 needles.

ABBREVIATIONS
C4B slip next 2 sts onto cable needle and hold at back of work, k2, then k2 from cable needle.
pfb purl into front and back of next st.
pkp [p1, k1, p1] into next st.
Also see page 10.

TO MAKE
With size 6 needles, cast on 81 sts.
Seed st row K1, [p1, k1] to end.
Rep this row 4 times more.
Inc row K1, pkp, k1, [p2, pfb, p2, k1, pkp, k1, pkp, k1] to end. *121 sts.*
1st row (right side) [K1, p1] 3 times, k4, * p1, [k1, p1] 5 times, k4; rep from * to last 6 sts, [p1, k1] 3 times.
2nd row [K1, p1] 3 times, p4, * p1, [k1, p1] 5 times, p4; rep from * to last 6 sts, [p1, k1] 3 times.
3rd row [K1, p1] 3 times, C4B, * p1, [k1, p1] 5 times, C4B; rep from * to last 6 sts, [p1, k1] 3 times.
4th row Rep 2nd row.
Shape beret
Inc row Seed st 6, M1, k4, M1, * seed st 11, M1, k4, M1; rep from * to last 6 sts, seed st 6. *137 sts.*
Next row Seed st 7, p4, * seed st 13, p4; rep from * to last 7 sts, seed st 7.
Next row Seed st 7, C4B, * seed st 13, C4B; rep from * to last 7 sts, seed st 7.
Next row Seed st 7, p4, * seed st 13, p4; rep from * to last 7 sts, seed st 7.
The last 4 rows show the inc sts on one right-side row and the cable crosses on the foll right-side row, keeping the seed st and cable sts correct as set and taking inc sts into seed st, cont to inc 1 st at each side of every 4-st cable on 3 foll 4th rows until the foll row has been worked:
Inc row (right side) Seed st 9, M1, k4, M1, * seed st 17, M1, k4, M1; rep from * to last 9 sts, seed st 9. *185 sts.*

a cabled beret with
continental chic

Keeping all sts correct, work 7 rows without further shaping.

Dec row (right side) Seed st 9, [k2tog, k2, ssk, seed st 17] 7 times, k2tog, k2, ssk, seed st 9. *169 sts.*

Next row Seed st 9, p4, [seed st 17, p4] 7 times, seed st 9.

Next row Seed st 9, C4B, [seed st 17, C4B] 7 times, seed st 9.

Next row Seed st 9, p4, [seed st 17, p4] 7 times, seed st 9.

Dec row (right side) Seed st 8, [k2tog, k2, ssk, seed st 15] 7 times, k2tog, k2, ssk, seed st 8. *153 sts.*

Cont in this way to dec 16 sts on every foll 4th row until 41 sts rem, ending with a dec row.

Next row K1, [p4, k1] 8 times.

Next row K1, [C4B, k1] 8 times.

Next row K1, [p4, k1] 8 times.

Dec row K2tog, [k2, k3tog] to last 4 sts, k2, k2tog. *25 sts.*

P 1 row.

Dec row K1, [k3tog] to end. *9 sts.*

P 1 row.

Dec row K1, [k2tog] 4 times. *5 sts.*

Do not cut off yarn.

STALK

Slip rem 5 sts onto a size 3 double-pointed needle and hold in left hand, then with right side facing, pull yarn firmly from last st to first st across wrong side, and k5.

With right side still facing, slide these 5 sts to the opposite end of the same needle, place needle in left hand, pull yarn tightly from last st to first st across wrong side, and k5.

Rep the last row 6 times more.

Leaving a 12in yarn end, cut the yarn, thread through sts, pull to gather, and secure. Using a blunt-ended yarn needle, pass the yarn down through the center of the stalk, then sew the seam down to the cast-on edge.

Teapot cozy

There was a period in my childhood when, at every teatime, no self-respecting teapot was without its pleated cozy. Usually these cozies were knitted in combinations of various shades, so in honor to my favorite beverage here is my take on the retro teapot cozy in a striking, clashing pairing of rust and pink.

SIZE
To fit a standard six-cup round "Brown Betty" teapot

MATERIALS
Debbie Bliss Rialto DK (100% extra-fine merino wool, approx 115 yd per 1¾oz/50g ball)
Two balls in each of fuchsia (A) and rust (B)
Pair of size 6 knitting needles

GAUGE
22 sts and 28 rows to 4in square over St st using size 6 needles.

ABBREVIATIONS
See page 10.

PATTERN NOTE
When working the pattern, the "puckers" are formed by pulling the yarn not in use across the wrong side of the work and twisting the two yarns together at the color change between the 2nd and 3rd stitches of every row.

SIDES (MAKE 2)
With size 6 needles and A, cast on 112 sts.
K 1 row.
Change to B and k 2 rows.
Now work in patt as follows:
1st row (right side) K2A, twist yarns together, [k9B, pull yarn A across back of work and k9A, pull yarn B across back of work] 6 times, k2B.
2nd row K2B, twist yarns together, [bring yarn B to front (wrong side) of work, take yarn A to back (right side) of work, k9A, pull yarn B across wrong side of work, bring yarn A to front (wrong side) of work, take yarn B to back (right side) of work, k9B, pull yarn A across wrong side of work] 6 times, k2A.
These 2 rows **form** the patt and are repeated.
Cont in patt until work measures 6in from cast-on edge, ending with a wrong-side row.
Shape top
Cont to twist yarns between 2nd and 3rd sts of every row and pull yarn not in use across wrong side of work and shape as follows:
1st dec row (right side) K2A, [with B, skp, k5B, k2tog B, with A, skp, k5A, k2tog A] 6 times, k2B.
Next row K2B, [k7A, k7B] 6 times, k2A.
2nd dec row K2A, [with B, skp, k3B, k2tog B, with A, skp, k3A, k2tog A] 6 times, k2B.
Next row K2B, [k5A, k5B] 6 times, k2A.

3rd dec row K2A, [with B, skp, k1B, k2tog B, with A, skp, k1A, k2tog A] 6 times, k2B.
Next row K2B, [k3A, k3B] 6 times, k2A.
4th dec row K2A, [with B, sl 1, k2tog, psso, with A, sl 1, k2tog, psso] 6 times, k2B.
Next row K2B, [k1A, k1B] 6 times, k2A. *16 sts.*
Next row [K2tog A, k2tog B] to end. *8 sts.*
Cut off yarns, thread both yarns through rem sts, pull to gather, and secure.

TO FINISH
Sew the two pieces together along the row-end edges, leaving gaps in the seams for the spout and the handle. Make a 1½in pompom using both yarns and sew to top of cozy.

keep your tea
steaming hot

Mug cozy

Whether I am sipping tea, coffee, chocolate, or any other hot beverage, I like to make sure my drink doesn't cool off too quickly and so a mug cozy is a great help in keeping it warm. Worked in a two-color slip stitch pattern in a double-knitting-weight yarn, you can either match the colors of your mug cozy to your teapot cozy or go for a different colorway altogether.

SIZE
To fit a straight-sided 4in tall mug with an external diameter of 3⅛in.

MATERIALS
Debbie Bliss Rialto DK (100% extra-fine merino wool, approx 115 yd per 1¾oz/50g ball)
Small amount in each of fuchsia (A) and rust (B)
Pair of size 6 knitting needles

GAUGE
25 sts and 52 rows to 4in square over patt using size 6 needles.

ABBREVIATIONS
wyib with yarn in back of work.
wyif with yarn in front of work.
Also see page 10.

COZY
With size 6 needles and A, cast on 63 sts.
K 1 row.
1st and 3rd rows (right side) With B, k3, [sl 1 wyib, k3] to end.
2nd and 4th rows With B k3, [sl 1 wyif, k3] to end.
5th and 6th rows With A, k to end.
These 6 rows **form** the patt and are repeated.
Cont in patt until work measures 3¼in from cast-on edge, ending with a 5th row.
Bind off knitwise in A.

TO FINISH
Sew together row-end edges at top and bottom, leaving a large opening in the seam for the handle.

101

Door draft stopper

Textured blackberry stitch, a braided cable and rib are a great pattern combination for this draft stopper worked in a practical dark gray in Rialto Aran, my soft but hardwearing extra-fine merino wool. Laying across the bottom of the door to block any cold gusts of air, it is the stylish solution to keeping the shivers away.

SIZE
Approximately 34in long

MATERIALS
Debbie Bliss Rialto Aran (100% extra-fine merino wool, approx 88 yd per 1¾oz/50g ball)
Three balls in charcoal
Size 8 circular knitting needle
Cable needle
5in x 35in piece of cotton fabric
Styrofoam beads for filling

GAUGE
25 sts and 24 rows to 4in square over patt using size 8 needles.

ABBREVIATIONS
C4B slip next 2 sts onto cable needle and hold at back of work, k2, then k2 from cable needle.
C4F slip next 2 sts onto cable needle and hold to front of work, k2, then k2 from cable needle.
kpk [k1, p1, k1] all into next st.

Also see page 10.

TO MAKE
With size 8 circular needle, cast on 228 sts.
1st row (right side) [P1, k2] twice, [p1, C4B, k2, p1, k2, p14, k2] 8 times, p1, C4B, k2, p1, [k2, p1] twice.
2nd row [K1, p2] twice, * k1, p6, k1, p2, k1, [kpk, p3tog] 3 times, k1, p2; rep from * 7 times more, k1, p6, k1, [p2, k1] twice.
3rd row [P1, k2] twice, [p1, k2, C4F, p1, k2, p14, k2] 8 times, p1, k2, C4F, p1, [k2, p1] twice.
4th row [K1, p2] twice, * k1, p6, k1, p2, k1, [p3tog, kpk] 3 times, k1, p2; rep from * 7 times more, k1, p6, k1, [p2, k1] twice.
These 4 rows **form** the patt and are repeated throughout.
Cont in patt until work measures 8in from cast-on edge, ending with a wrong-side row.
Bind off in patt.

LINER
Fold the fabric piece in half lengthwise, then taking a ⅝in seam allowance, sew together the long edges to form a tube. Sew together one short end. Fill the tube with styrofoam beads, then stitch across the open end of the tube.

TO FINISH
Sew cast-on edge to bound-off edge. With seam lying centrally, sew together one short end. Insert the filled liner and sew the remaining short end closed.

block out chilly
fall breezes

Striped gloves
Knitted in simple stockinette stitch, I have kept the fingers of these gloves plain in order to make them easy to knit. So the stripes are worked on the main part of the hand and, for added interest, continue on the turned back cuff. I like the sophistication of the citrus brights against the dark gray base color but there are plenty more three-color combinations that would work well; try pastel shades for completely different look.

SIZE
To fit small/medium (medium/large) hands

MATERIALS
Debbie Bliss Rialto 4-ply (100% extra-fine merino wool, approx 110 yd per 1¾oz/ 50g ball)
One ball in each of gray (A), citrus (B), and orange (C)
Pair each of sizes 2 and 3 knitting needles

GAUGE
28 sts and 36 rows to 4in square over St st using size 3 needles.

ABBREVIATIONS
See page 10.

RIGHT GLOVE
** With size 3 needles and A, cast 58 (66) sts.
Cont in stripes of 2 rows A, 2 rows B, 2 rows A, 2 rows C throughout.
Rib row [K1, p1] to end.
This row **forms** rib.
Rib 23 rows more.
Change to size 2 needles.
Work 24 rows more.
Change to size 3 needles.
Beg with a k row, work in St st.
Work 14 rows. **
Thumb shaping
Next row (right side) K29 (33), M1, k3, M1, k to end.
Work 3 rows.
Next row K29 (33), M1, k5, M1, k to end.
P 1 row.
Next row K29 (33), M1, k7, M1, k to end.
P 1 row.
Next row K29 (33), M1, k9, M1, k to end.
P 1 row.
Cont to inc 2 sts as set on every right-side row until there are 74 (84) sts.
P 1 row.
Cont in A only.

Divide for thumb
Next row (right side) K48 (54), turn, cast on 2 sts.
Next row P21 (23) sts.
Work 18 rows in St st.
Next row K1, [k2tog] to end. *11 (12) sts.*
Next row P1, [p2tog] to last 0 (1) st, p0 (1).
Cut off yarn, thread through rem 6 (7) sts, pull tightly to gather, and sew seam.
With right side facing and continuing stripe sequence, join yarn to base of thumb, k to end. *55 (63) sts.*
Work 15 rows, so ending 2 rows C (A).
Cont in A only.
*** **Divide for fingers**
First finger
Next row K35 (41), turn and cast on 2 sts.
Next row P17 (19), turn.
Work 22 rows in St st.
Next row K1, [k2tog] to end.
Next row P1, [p2tog] to last 0 (1) st, p0 (1).
Cut off yarn, thread through rem 5 (6) sts, pull tightly to gather, and sew seam.
Second finger
With right side facing, join yarn to base of first finger, pick up and k 2 sts from base of first finger, k7 (8), turn, cast on 2 sts.

Next row P18 (20), turn.

Work 26 rows in St st.

Next row [K2tog] to end.

Next row P1, [p2tog] to last 0 (1) st, p0 (1).

Cut off yarn, thread through rem 5 (6) sts, pull tightly to gather, and sew seam.

Third finger

With right side facing, join yarn to base of second finger, pick up and k 2 sts from base of second finger, k7 (8), turn, cast on 2 sts.

Next row P18 (20), turn.

Work 22 rows in St st.

Next row [K2tog] to end.

Next row P1, [p2tog] to last 0 (1) st, p0 (1).

Cut off yarn, thread through rem 5 (6) sts, pull tightly to gather, and sew seam.

Fourth finger

With right side facing, join yarn to base of third finger, pick up and k 2 sts from base of third finger, k6 (6), turn.

Next row P14 (14).

Work 16 rows in St st.

Next row [K2tog] to end.

Next row P1, [p2tog] to end.

Cut off yarn, thread through rem 4 sts, pull tightly to gather, and sew seam, reversing first 24 rows for cuff.

LEFT GLOVE

Work as given for Right Glove from ** to **.

Thumb shaping

Next row K25 (29), M1, k3, M1, k to end.

Work 3 rows.

Next row K25 (29), M1, k5, M1, k to end.

P 1 row.

Next row K25 (29), M1, k7, M1, k to end.

P 1 row.

Next row K25 (29), M1, k9, M1, k to end.

P 1 row.

Cont to inc 2 sts as set on every right-side row until there are 74 (84) sts on needle.

P 1 row.

Divide for thumb

Next row K44 (50), turn, cast on 2 sts.

Next row P21 (23) sts.

Work 18 rows St st.

Next row K1, [k2tog] to end. *11 (12) sts.*

Next row P1, [p2tog] to last 0 (1) st, p0 (1).

Cut off yarn, thread through rem 6 (7) sts, pull tightly to gather, and sew seam.

With right side facing, join yarn to base of thumb, k to end. *55 (63) sts.*

Work 15 rows, ending 2 rows C (A).

Cont in A only.

Complete as for Right Glove from *** to end.

Pumpkin pincushion

As a reminder that knitting can be incredible fun, work this pumpkin pincushion as a Halloween gift for a crafter friend. But if pumpkins aren't their thing, this same pattern could be knitted in shades of red to make either an apple or a tomato.

SIZE

Approximately 3½in tall x 3½in in diameter, including stalk

MATERIALS

Debbie Bliss Rialto DK (100% extra-fine merino wool, approx 115 yd per 1¾oz/50g ball) One ball in orange (A) and a small amount in green (B) Pair of size 5 knitting needles Two size 5 double-pointed knitting needles Washable toy stuffing

GAUGE

25 sts and 32 rows to 4in square over St st using size 5 needles.

ABBREVIATIONS

See page 10.

PUMPKIN

With size 5 needles and A, cast on 7 sts.
1st row [Kfb] 7 times. *14 sts.*
2nd row Purl.
3rd row [K1, M1, k1] 7 times. *21 sts.*
4th row [P1, k1, p1] 7 times.
5th row [K1, M1, p1, M1, k1] 7 times. *35 sts.*
6th row [P2, k1, p2] 7 times.
7th row [K1, M1, k1, p1, k1, M1, k1] 7 times. *49 sts.*
8th row [P3, k1, p3] 7 times.
9th row [K3, p1, k3] 7 times.
10th row Rep 8th row.
11th row [K1, M1, k2, p1, k2, M1, k1] 7 times. *63 sts.*
12th row [P4, k1, p4] 7 times.
13th row [K4, p1, k4] 7 times.
14th row Rep 12th row.
15th row [K1, M1, k3, p1, k3, M1, k1] 7 times. *77 sts.*
16th row [P5, k1, p5] 7 times.
17th row [K5, p1, k5] 7 times.
18th row Rep 16th row.
19th row Rep 17th row.
20th row Rep 16th row.
21st row [K2tog, k3, p1, k3, k2tog] 7 times. *63 sts.*
22nd–24th rows Rep 12th–14th rows.
25th row [K2tog, k2, p1, k2, k2tog] 7 times. *49 sts.*
26th–28th rows Rep 8th–10th rows.
29th row [K2tog, k1, p1, k1, k2tog] 7 times. *35 sts.*
30th row [P2, k1, p2] 7 times.
31st row [K2tog, p1, k2tog] 7 times. *21 sts.*

32nd row [P1, k1, p1] 7 times.
33rd row [Sl 1, k2tog, psso] 7 times. *7 sts.*
Cut off yarn, thread through sts, pull to gather, and secure.

LEAVES AND STALK

With size 5 needles and B, cast on 54 sts.
1st row [K3, sl 1, k2tog, psso, k3] 6 times. *42 sts.*
2nd, 4th, and 6th rows Purl.
3rd row [K2, sl 1, k2tog, psso, k2] 6 times. *30 sts.*
5th row [K1, sl 1, k2tog, psso, k1] 6 times. *18 sts.*
7th row [Sl 1, k2tog, psso] 6 times. *6 sts.*
8th row P1, p2tog, p2tog, p1. *4 sts.*
Change to size 5 double-pointed needles.
Next row K4.
Next row Keeping right side facing, transfer needle into left hand, slide sts to opposite end of needle, pull yarn tightly across wrong side, and k4.
Repeat the last row 6 times more.
Cut off yarn, thread through sts, pull to gather, and secure. Thread yarn down through the stalk and sew together row-end edges.

TO FINISH

Sew side seam on pumpkin, leaving a 1½in gap. Stuff firmly and sew gap in seam closed.
With a length of B in a blunt-ended yarn needle, wind yarn along the 7 purl stitch gulleys, securing yarn at top and bottom of pumpkin. Arrange leaves and stalk on the top of the pumpkin and stitch in place.
Work a few sts in B at the base of the pumpkin.

cheery covers for your
mp3 player or pda

Gadget covers

Knitted covers in bold stripes are a colorful way of making sure you can find your Blackberry or iPod in a cluttered bag. The ribbed stitch pattern expands so the cover will fit a variety of different-sized gadgets. It is a brilliant way of using up your scraps of yarn as one cover takes only a very small amount of each color. So try out lots of colorways to make each gadget cover completely unique.

SIZE
Approximately 2in x 4¼in

MATERIALS
Debbie Bliss Baby Cashmerino (55% merino wool, 33% microfiber, 12% cashmere, approx 137 yd per 1¾oz/50g ball)
Small amount in each of brown, peach, green, turquoise, gray, rust, and gold
Pair of size 2 knitting needles

GAUGE
32 sts and 36 rows to 4in square over rib using size 2 needles.

ABBREVIATIONS
See page 10.

TIP
You can use these basic instructions to make a cover for any version of the MP3 player or PDA; just adjust the cast-on stitch count and number of rows.

IPOD COVER
With size 2 needles and brown, cast on 33 sts.
1st row (right side) K1, [p1, k1] to end.
2nd row P1, [k1, p1] to end.
These 2 rows **form** the rib and are repeated.
Work in rib in stripes as follows: 4 rows brown, 2 rows gold, 2 rows peach, 3 rows turquoise, 2 rows gray, 1 row rust, 3 rows green, 2 rows brown, 3 rows gold, 2 rows peach, 2 rows rust, 1 row gray, 2 rows brown, 4 rows turquoise, 1 row green, 3 rows peach, 3 rows brown.
Bind off in brown.

TO FINISH
Sew together row-end edges matching stripes. Sew in all yarn ends neatly.

SIZE
Approximately 4¾in x 2in

MATERIALS
Oddments of Debbie Bliss Baby Cashmerino in each of brown, pink, green, turquoise, gray, rust, red, and gold
Pair of size 3 knitting needles

GAUGE
30 sts and 35 rows to 4in square over rib using size 3 needles.

BLACKBERRY COVER
With size 3 needles and brown, cast on 33 sts.
Work rib as given for iPod Cover, but working the stripe sequence as follows:
4 rows brown, 3 rows pink, 2 rows green, 4 rows turquoise, 1 row gray, 2 rows brown, 2 rows rust, 2 rows red, 1 row pink, 2 rows gold, 2 rows brown, 3 rows green, 1 row rust, 2 rows gray, 2 rows turquoise, 1 row red, 3 rows pink, 1 row gold, 4 rows brown.
Bind off in brown.

TO FINISH
As iPod Cover.

Slippers

Knitted all in one piece, these slippers are worked in a supersoft camel and extra-fine merino blend yarn called Fez—a little bit of luxury for your feet. The duck egg blue edging contrasts the chocolate brown garter stitch and, like the pompoms, adds a bit of decorative detail.

SIZES

To fit women's shoe sizes 6–7 (7–8)

MATERIALS

Debbie Bliss Fez (85% extra-fine merino wool, 15% camel, approx 110 yd per 1¾oz/50g ball)

Two balls in chocolate (A) and one ball in duck egg (B)

Pair of size 7 knitting needles

Size 7 circular knitting needle

GAUGE

21 sts and 38 rows to 4in square over garter st using size 7 needles.

ABBREVIATIONS

s2togkp slip 2 sts tog, k1, then pass 2 slipped sts over.
Also see page 10.

SLIPPER (MAKE 2)

1st side With size 7 needles and A, cast on 6 sts.
K 1 row.
Next row Cast on 7 sts, k to end. *13 sts.*
K 2 rows. Leave sts on needle.
2nd side With size 7 needles and A, cast on 6 sts.
K 2 rows.
Next row Cast on 7 sts, k to end. *13 sts.*
K 1 row.
Joining row (right side) K across 13 sts of 2nd side, cast on 7 sts, then k across 13 sts of 1st side.
Shape heel of sole
Next row K13, p1, k5, p1, k13.
Next row K14, M1, k5, M1, k14. *35 sts.*
Next row K13, p1, k7, p1, k13.
Next row K14, M1, k7, M1, k14. *37 sts.*
Next row K13, p1, k9, p1, k13.
Next row K14, M1, k9, M1, k14. *39 sts.*
Next row K13, p1, k11, p1, k13.
Next row K14, M1, k11, M1, k14. *41 sts.*
Place markers at each end of next row.
Next row K13, p1, k13, p1, k13.
Next row K41.
Rep the last 2 rows (from markers) 26 (30) times more, so ending with a wrong-side row.
Shape toe
Next row K1, ssk, k to last 3 sts, k2tog, k1. *39 sts.*
Next row K12, p1, k13, p1, k12.
K 1 row.
Next row K12, p1, k13, p1, k12.
Next row K1, ssk, k to last 3 sts, k2tog, k1. *37 sts.*
Next row K11, p1, k13, p1, k11.
K 1 row.
Next row K11, p1, k13, p1, k11.
Next row K1, [ssk, k9] twice, k2tog, k9, k2tog, k1. *33 sts.*

Next row K10, p1, k11, p1, k10.
K 1 row.
Next row K10, p1, k11, p1, k10.
Next row K1, ssk, k to last 3 sts, k2tog, k1. *31 sts.*
Next row K9, p1, k11, p1, k9.
K 1 row.
Next row K9, p1, k11, p1, k9.
Next row K1, [ssk, k7] twice, k2tog, k7, k2tog, k1. *27 sts.*
Next row K8, p1, k9, p1, k8.
Next row K1, ssk, k6, ssk, k5, k2tog, k6, k2tog, k1. *23 sts.*
Next row K7, [p1, k7] twice.
Next row K1, ssk, k5, ssk, k3, k2tog, k5, k2tog, k1. *19 sts.*
Next row K6, p1, k5, p1, k6.
Next row K1, [ssk] twice, s2togkp, k3, s2togkp, [k2tog] twice, k1. *11 sts.*
Next row K3, [p1, k3] twice.
Next row K1, [ssk] twice, k1, [k2tog] twice, k1.
Bind off knitwise.

EDGING

To form top seam, sew together row-end edges from toe bound-off edge for approximately 4¼in (or as required).

With right side facing, size 7 circular needle and B, pick up and k one st in every alt row-end all around top edge of slipper. Bind off knitwise.

Sew together cast-on edges of 1st and 2nd sides and edging to form back seam and sew row-ends of sides to heel cast-on sts.

TO FINISH

With B, make two pompoms and sew to top of slippers.

snuggly slippers
for toasty toes

Cabled bag
A hot pink bag will add a splash of bright color to your fall wardrobe. Knitted in my super-soft, super-chunky Como yarn, the thickness of the wool makes the scale of the oversized cable and bobbles big and bold. Knitted from the base of the bag upward, the cable runs up the side of the bag and then continues to forms the handles. To finish the bag, it is lined with a matching bright tartan fabric.

SIZE
Approximately 13¾in x 9½in
x 4in (see NOTE)

MATERIALS
Debbie Bliss Como (90% wool,
10% cashmere, approx 46 yd
per 1¾oz/50g ball)
Seven balls in fuchsia
Pair of size 13 knitting needles
Cable needle
1⅛yd of cotton fabric for lining
3½in x 12½in piece of
cardboard for base

GAUGE
9 sts and 14 rows to 4in square
over St st using size 13 needles.

NOTE
The size given above is the
approximate external size. As
the yarn is bulky, the internal
size will be smaller.

ABBREVIATIONS
MB (make bobble) [k1, p1] twice into next st,
turn, k4, turn, p4, turn, k4, turn, sl 2, k2tog,
pass 2 slipped sts over.
C3B slip next st onto cable needle and hold at
back of work, k2, then k1 from cable needle.
C3F slip next 2 sts onto cable needle and hold to
front of work, k1, then k2 from cable needle.
C3FP slip next 2 sts onto cable needle and hold
to front of work, p1, then k2 from cable needle.
C3BP slip next st onto cable needle and hold at
back of work, k2, then p1 from cable needle.
C4B slip next 2 sts onto cable needle and hold
at back of work, k2, then k2 from cable needle.
C4F slip next 2 sts onto cable needle and hold
to front of work, k2, then k2 from cable needle.
Also see page 10.

CENTER PANEL (WORKED OVER 15 STS)
1st row P5, k2, MB, k2, p5.
2nd row K5, p5, k5.
3rd row P5, MB, k3, MB, p5.
4th row K5, p5, k5.
5th and 6th rows Rep 1st and 2nd rows.

7th row P4, C3B, p1, C3F, p4.
8th row K4, p3, k1, p3, k4.
9th row P3, C3B, p1, k1, p1, C3F, p3.
10th row K3, p3, k1, p1, k1, p3, k3.
11th row P2, C3B, [p1, k1] twice, p1, C3F, p2.
12th row K2, p3, [k1, p1] twice, k1, p3, k2.
13th row P1, C3B, [p1, k1] 3 times, p1, C3F, p1.
14th row K1, p3, [k1, p1] 3 times, k1, p3, k1.
15th row C3B, [p1, k1] 4 times, p1, C3F.
16th row P3, [k1, p1] 4 times, k1, p3.
17th row K2, [p1, k1] 5 times, p1, k2.
18th row P2, [k1, p1] 5 times, k1, p2.
19th row C3FP, [p1, k1] 4 times, p1, C3BP.
20th row K1, p2, [k1, p1] 4 times, k1, p2, k1.
21st row P1, C3FP, [p1, k1] 3 times, p1, C3BP, p1.
22nd row K2, p2, [k1, p1] 3 times, k1, p2, k2.
23rd row P2, C3FP, [p1, k1] twice, p1, C3BP, p2.
24th row K3, p2, [k1, p1] twice, k1, p2, k3.
25th row P3, C3FP, p1, k1, p1, C3BP, p3.
26th row K4, p2, k1, p1, k1, p2, k4.
27th row P4, C3FP, p1, C3BP, p4.
28th row K5, p5, k5.
29th–34th rows Rep 1st–6th rows.
These 34 rows **form** the center panel.

BACK AND FRONT (BOTH ALIKE)
With size 13 needles, cast on 45 sts.
K 1 row.
Next row (wrong side) K9, p4, k19, p4, k9.
Work in patt as follows:
1st row (right side) [K1, p1] 3 times, k9, work across 15 sts of 1st row of center panel, k9, [p1, k1] 3 times.
2nd row P1, [k1, p1] 3 times, k2, p4, k2, work across 2nd row of center panel, k2, p4, k2, p1, [k1, p1] 3 times.
3rd row P1, [k1, p1] 3 times, k2, C4F, k2, work across 3rd row of center panel, k2, C4B, k2, p1, [k1, p1] 3 times.
4th row K1, [p1, k1] 3 times, k2, p4, k2, work across 4th row of center panel, k2, p4, k2, k1, [p1, k1] 3 times.
These 4 rows **form** the patt for the 4-st cable with seed st at each side and set the position for the center panel.
Cont in patt working correct panel rows until all 34 rows of center panel have been worked.
Next row K9, C4F, k19, C4B, k9.
Next row K9, p4, k19, p4, k9.
Next row K to end.
Next row K9, p4, k19, p4, k9.
Next row Bind off 7 sts, with one st on needle after bind-off, k next st, C4F, k2, leave these 8 sts on a holder, bind off next 15 sts, with one st on needle after bind-off, k next st, C4B, k2, bind off rem 7 sts and fasten off, leave second set of 8 sts on the needle.
Handles
With wrong side facing, rejoin yarn to 8 sts on needle and work as follows:
** **1st row** (wrong side) K2, p4, k2.
2nd row K to end.
3rd row K2, p4, k2.
4th row K2, C4B, k2.
Rep the last 4 rows until strap measures 10in, ending with a right-side row.

Bind off **.
With wrong side facing and size 13 needles, rejoin yarn to 8 sts on holder and work from ** to **, working C4F instead of C4B.

GUSSET
With size 13 needles, cast on 13 sts.
K 4 rows.
1st row (right side) K1, [p1, k1] 6 times.
2nd row P1, [k1, p1] 6 times.
3rd row Rep 2nd row.
4th row Rep 1st row.
These 4 rows **form** the seed st.
Cont in moss st until gusset measures 33½in, ending with a wrong-side row.
K 4 rows.
Bind off.

LINING
Using the knitted pieces as templates (excluding handles) and adding ⅝in for seams all around, cut out lining fabric for back, front, and gusset. Mark the handle positions on the back and front linings. Pin and baste the gusset to back and front around two short sides and one long edge, then stitch the seams, taking a ⅝in seam allowance. Press ⅝in onto wrong side around top edge. Cut out two pieces of lining fabric 21¼in long by 2¾in wide for handle linings. Cover the cardboard base in fabric.

TO FINISH
Stitch gusset to back and front, starting and finishing at top edge. Sew together bound-off edges of handles. For handle linings, press ⅝in onto wrong side along both long edges, then slipstitch to center of wrong side of knitted handles. Place lining inside bag and slipstitch top edge in place, enclosing ends of handle lining. Slip covered cardboard base inside bag.

Winter

Chunky scarf
This scarf is generously long but knitted in Como, a super-chunky blend of merino wool and cashmere, and worked on large needles it really can be knitted up within one week. And because the weight of the Como yarn means each stitch is well defined, the aran-style pattern of chevrons, seed stitch, and bobbles really stands out.

SIZE
Approximately 8¾in wide x 71in long

MATERIALS
Debbie Bliss Como (90% wool, 10% cashmere, approx 46 yd per 1¾oz/50g ball)
Seven balls in gray
Pair of size 10½ knitting needles
Cable needle

GAUGE
10 sts and 15 rows to 4in square over St st using size 10½ needles.

ABBREVIATIONS
C3BP slip next st onto cable needle and hold at back of work, k2, then p1 from cable needle.
C3FP slip next 2 sts onto cable needle and hold to front of work, p1, then k2 from cable needle.
MB (make bobble) k into front, back, and front of next st, turn and p3, turn and k3, turn and p1, p2tog, turn and k2tog.
T5BP slip next 3 sts onto cable needle and hold at back of work, k2, then p1, k2 from cable needle.
Also see page 10.

TO MAKE
With size 10½ needles, cast on 27 sts.
1st row (right side) [K1, p1] twice, k3, p4, k2, p1, k2, p4, k3, [p1, k1] twice.
2nd row [P1, k1] twice, k7, p2, k1, p2, k7, [k1, p1] twice.
3rd row [P1, k1] twice, p7, T5BP, p7, [k1, p1] twice.
4th row [K1, p1] twice, k7, p2, k1, p2, k7, [p1, k1] twice.
5th row [K1, p1] twice, p6, C3BP, MB, C3FP, p6, [p1, k1] twice.
6th row [P1, k1] twice, k6, p2, k1, p1, k1, p2, k6, [k1, p1] twice.
7th row [P1, k1] twice, p5, C3BP, k1, p1, k1, C3FP, p5, [k1, p1] twice.
8th row [K1, p1] twice, k5, p2, k1, [p1, k1] twice, p2, k5, [p1, k1] twice.
9th row [K1, p1] twice, p4, C3BP, k1, [p1, k1] twice, C3FP, p4, [p1, k1] twice.
10th row [P1, k1] twice, k4, p2, k1, [p1, k1] 3 times, p2, k4, [k1, p1] twice.
11th row [P1, k1] twice, p3, C3BP, k1, [p1, k1] 3 times, C3FP, p3, [k1, p1] twice.
12th row [K1, p1] twice, k3, p2, k1, [p1, k1] 4 times, p2, k3, [p1, k1] twice.
13th row [K1, p1] twice, p2, C3BP, k1, [p1, k1] 4 times, C3FP, p2, [p1, k1] twice.
14th row [P1, k1] twice, k2, p2, k1, [p1, k1] 5 times, p2, k2, [k1, p1] twice.
15th row [P1, k1] twice, p1, C3BP, k1, [p1, k1] 5 times, C3FP, p1, [k1, p1] twice.
16th row [K1, p1] twice, k1, p2, k1, [p1, k1] 6 times, p2, k1, [p1, k1] twice.
These 16 rows **form** the cable and bobble patt with seed stitch at each side and are repeated 15 times more.
Bind off.

*a plump pillow
in perfect plaid*

Tartan pillow

Guaranteed to brighten up any chair, this tartan pillow cover is worked in stockinette stitch using the Fair Isle method of colorwork with the bright verticals embroidered on afterward for ease. The back of the pillow cover is plain with a central button opening. The entire cover is knitted in Rialto Aran, my pure merino wool aran-weight yarn, so it knits up as quickly as possible.

SIZE
Approximately 14in square

MATERIALS
Debbie Bliss Rialto Aran (100% extra-fine merino wool, approx 88 yd per 1¾oz/50g ball)
Four balls in navy (A), two 50g balls in red (B), and one 50g ball in gold (C)
Pair each of sizes 7 and 8 knitting needles
3 buttons
14in square pillow form

GAUGE
21 sts and 28 rows to 4in square over St st using size 7 needles.

ABBREVIATIONS
yo2 yarn over twice (yarn around right-hand needle twice to make 2 new sts).
Also see page 10.

CHART NOTES
When working from chart (see page 124), work right-side rows from right to left as follows—k2 edge sts, [k across 20 sts of repeat] 3 times, then k 15 edge sts; and work wrong-side rows from left to right as follows—p 15 edge sts, [p across 20 sts of repeat] 3 times, then p2 edge sts.
Work the first 2 rows, then work the 28-row repeat twice, then work the last 20 rows (78 rows worked in total).
Do not work the vertical stitches marked in C, as these will be worked in duplicate stitch on the finished knitted cover; when knitting from the chart, work these stitches in either A or B, whichever is appropriate.

TO MAKE

With size 7 needles and A, cast on 77 sts.

K 6 rows.

P 1 row.

Buttonhole row (right side) K11, [k2tog, yo2, ssk, k21] twice, k2tog, yo2, ssk, k12.

Next row P, working [p1, p1 tbl] into each yo2.

Beg with a k row, cont in St st until work measures 3½in, ending with a k row.

Change to size 8 needles.

Foldline row (wrong side) Knit.

Beg with k row, work 78 rows in St st from chart, see Chart Notes.

Change to size 7 needles and work in A only.

Foldline row (right side) Purl.

Beg with a p row, work in St st until cover measures 10¾in from foldline row, ending with a k row.

K 4 rows.

Bind off knitwise on wrong side.

TO FINISH

Work the yarn C vertical lines in duplicate stitch following the chart.

Fold the larger part of the cover back onto the wrong side along the foldline row and sew the side seams. Fold the remaining cover back along the foldline row and stitch the side seams.

Sew on the buttons to correspond with the buttonholes.

Slip the pillow form into the cover and fasten the buttons.

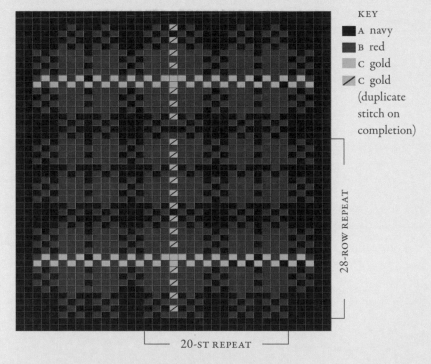

KEY

A navy

B red

C gold

C gold (duplicate stitch on completion)

28-ROW REPEAT

20-ST REPEAT

Christmas napkin rings
Red napkin rings on crisp white linen—perfect!

Simple knitted garter stitch strips are looped around each other, like a Russian wedding ring, to prove the maxim that less is more. These napkin rings bring an easy elegance to your Christmas table setting, and take only a few minutes to make.

SIZE
Each three-ring napkin ring will fit over a rolled standard-sized napkin

MATERIALS
Debbie Bliss Rialto 4-Ply (100% extra-fine merino wool, approx 110 yd per 1¾oz/50g ball)
One ball in red (see NOTE)
Pair of size 2 knitting needles

GAUGE
32 sts to 4in over garter st using size 2 needles.

ABBREVIATIONS
See page 10.

NOTE
Small amounts of leftover yarn can be used as each ring weighs only approximately 3 grams.

NAPKIN RING STRIPS (MAKE 3)
Each napkin ring is made from three garter stitch strips. Make each of the strips as follows:
With size 2 needles, cast on 45 sts.
K 4 rows, so ending with a right-side row.
Bind off knitwise.

TO FINISH
Sew together row-end edges of one strip to form a ring. Thread the second strip through the first ring and sew together the row-end edges to form a ring. Thread the third strip through the other two strips and sew together the row-end edges to form a ring.

KEY
■ 1ST RING
■ 2ND RING
■ 3RD RING

Booties trio

These three pairs of booties would make the most perfect gift set for any new baby. All three styles of booties are worked from the same basic pattern: striped top with a roll-over cuff, striped sides with turned-up tops, or lace-edged with a bow. Smart or pretty, there is a pair for every occasion. Each design is knitted in Baby Cashmerino, my supersoft cashmere, merino, and microfiber blend.

SIZE
To fit ages 3–6 months

MATERIALS
Debbie Bliss Baby Cashmerino
(55% merino wool, 33% microfiber, 12% cashmere, approx
137 yd per 1¾oz/50g ball)
One ball in each of red (A) and
gray (B)
Pair each of sizes 2 and 3
knitting needles

GAUGE
28 sts and 37 rows to 4in
square over St st using size
2 needles.

ABBREVIATIONS
See page 10.

NOTE
One 50g ball of each color will
make all three pairs of booties.

BOOTIES WITH STRIPED INSTEP
** With size 2 needles and A, cast on 36 sts.
K 1 row.
1st row (right side) K1, yo, k16, yo, [k1, yo]
twice, k16, yo, k1.
2nd and all wrong-side rows K to end,
working k1 tbl into each yo of previous row.
3rd row K2, yo, k16, yo, k2, yo, k3, yo, k16,
yo, k2.
5th row K3, yo, k16, yo, [k4, yo] twice, k16,
yo, k3.
7th row K4, yo, k16, yo, k5, yo, k6, yo, k16,
yo, k4.
9th row K5, yo, k16, yo, [k7, yo] twice, k16,
yo, k5.
11th row K22, yo, k8, yo, k9, yo, k22. *64 sts.*
12th row Rep 2nd row. **
Beg with a k row, work 10 rows in St st.
Shape instep
Next row With A, k36, skp, turn.
Next row With A, sl 1, p8, p2tog, turn.
Cont in stripes of 2 rows B and 2 rows A and
work as follows:
Next row Sl 1, k8, skp, turn.

Next row Sl 1, p8, p2tog, turn.
Rep the last 2 rows 7 times more.
Cont in A only.
Next row Sl 1, k to end.
Next row P17, p2tog, p8, p2tog tbl, p17. *44 sts.*
Rib row [K1, p1] to end.
Rep the last row 9 times more.
Change to size 3 needles.
Work 12 rows more in rib.
Bind off in rib.
Sew back seam and sole seam.

BOOTIES WITH STRIPED FOOT

Work as given for Booties with Striped Instep from ** to **.

Beg with a k row, work 5 rows in St st.

Next row (wrong side) [P next st tog with corresponding st 3 rows below] to end.

Beg with a k row, work 10 rows in St st, working in stripes of 2 rows B, 2 rows A.

Cont in A only.

Shape instep

Next row K36, skp, turn.

Next row Sl 1, p8, p2tog, turn.

Next row Sl 1, k8, skp, turn.

Rep the last 2 rows 7 times more, then work first of the 2 rows again.

Next row Sl 1, k to end.

Next row P17, p2tog, p8, p2tog tbl, p17. *44 sts.*

Rib row [K1, p1] to end.

Rep the last row 9 times more.

Rib 2 rows B, 2 rows A, and 2 rows B.

With B, bind off in rib.

Sew back seam and sole seam.

BOOTIES WITH LACY TOP

With B, work as given for Booties with Striped Instep from ** to **.

With A, k 2 rows.

With B, beg with a k row, work 8 rows in St st.

With A, k 2 rows.

Cont in B only.

Shape instep

Next row K36, skp, turn.

Next row Sl 1, p8, p2tog, turn.

Next row Sl 1, k8, skp, turn.

Rep the last 2 rows 7 times more, then work first of the 2 rows again.

Next row Sl 1, k to end.

Next row P17, p2tog, p8, p2tog tbl, p17. *44 sts.*

Change to size 3 needles and cont in patt as follows:

1st row K2, [k2tog, yo, k1, yo, skp, k2] to end.

2nd row P to end.

3rd row K1, [k2tog, yo, k3, yo, skp] to to last st, k1.

4th row P to end.

These 4 rows **form** the patt.

Patt 12 rows more.

With A, k 1 row.

With A, bind off knitwise.

Sew back seam and sole seam.

Using 2 strands of B, make a twisted cord 18in long for each bootie. Thread through first row of eyelet holes to tie at center front.

Pompom garland

There really is nothing simpler—or more satifysing—than making pompoms. In cool white, these giant pompoms remind me of oversized snowballs; they make the simplest but most stylish seasonal decorations for winter time. Get the kids to help with winding the wool around the pompom maker then, once they are finished, string each fluffy pompom onto a strand of yarn.

SIZE
Each pompom measures
3½in in diameter

MATERIALS
Debbie Bliss Rialto DK (100% extra-fine merino wool, approx 115 yd per 1¾oz/50g ball)
Five balls in white
Pompom maker or cardboard for circles
Blunt-ended yarn needle
Scissors

NOTE
Each pompom takes one 50g ball of yarn.

TO MAKE
If using cardboard, cut two identical cardboard circles 3½in in diameter.
Cut a hole 2in in diameter in the center of each one and hold the circles together. Thread a blunt-ended yarn needle with yarn and wind it continually through the center and around the outer edges until the hole has closed.
Insert the tips of the scissors between the two circles and cut the yarn around the circles. Tie a piece of yarn tightly between the two circles and remove the cardboard.

TO FINISH
With a yarn needle, thread the pompoms onto a length of yarn and make a loop at each end. Drape the line of pompoms between two points.

Doorstop

Keep the household traffic flowing with this great doorstop. Knitted in tweed stitch—a sturdy variation of my favorite seed stitch—and made from an organic cotton in an aran weight, this robust fabric can put up with a lot of wear and tear.

SIZE
Approximately 6¼in in each direction (this will change slightly when the doorstop is filled)

MATERIALS
Debbie Bliss Eco Aran DK (100% organic cotton, approx 99 yd per 1¾oz/50g ball)
One ball in silver
Pair of size 7 knitting needles
Approximately 20oz of small dried peas or beans

GAUGE
24 sts and 36 rows to 4in square over patt using size 7 needles.

ABBREVIATIONS
yb yarn to back of work between two needles
yf yarn to front of work between two needles.
pwise purlwise
Also see page 10.

DOORSTOP
With size 7 needles, cast on 39 sts.
1st row (right side) K1, [yf, sl 1 pwise, yb, k1] to end.
2nd row P2, [yb, sl 1 pwise, yf, p1] to last st, p1.
These 2 rows **form** the patt and are repeated throughout.
Cont in patt until work measures approximately 12½in from cast-on edge, ending with a right-side row.
Bind off, work p2tog across the row, ending with p1.

LOOP
Cut three lengths of yarn 12in long.
Fold each strand of yarn in half and braid the doubled yarn.
Fold the braid in half to form a loop and secure the ends together.

TO FINISH
Sew cast-on and bound-off edges together forming a tube (this seam will run along the center of the base of the doorstop).
Fold tube in half with the base seam lying centrally and sew the seam from fold to fold (this seam will run across the front of the base of the doorstop).
Refold the tube to form the final shape, and with the braided loop at the fold (top of doorstop), sew the seam from the fold toward the original base seam, leaving approximately 1½in of the seam open.
Fill doorstop with the dried peas or beans and sew the opening closed.

*hold the door
with this
functional stopper*

*celebrate and spell out
the yuletide season*

Noel letters

This knitted "noel" could take center stage in your festive decorations year after year and become part of your family's Christmas customs. Backed by felt and stiffened with cardboard, the letters are worked in a traditional Scandinavian style of Fair Isle in my pure wool Rialto 4-Ply. You don't have to go for green; each of the letters could be knitted up in a different color if you wanted to use up leftovers from your stash.

SIZE
The letters "n," "o," and "e" are approximately 3¾in tall, and the letter "l" is 5¾in tall.

MATERIALS
Debbie Bliss Rialto 4-Ply (100% extra-fine merino wool, approx 110 yd per 1¾oz/50g ball)
One ball in each of sage green (A) and ecru (B)
Pair of size 2 needles
12in square of red felt
Cardboard
Double-sided adhesive tape

GAUGE
32 sts and 36 rows to 4in square over St st using size 2 needles.

ABBREVIATIONS
See page 11.

NOTES
All letters are made from straight strips using size 2 needles and are worked from charts.
Read right-side (k) rows from right to left and wrong-side (p) rows from left to right.

LETTER "N"
With A, cast on 21 sts.
Beg with a k row, work 35 rows in St st from right-hand side of chart 1 (see page 138), so ending with a k row.
Leave sts on a holder.
With A, cast on 21 sts.
Beg with a k row, work 35 rows in St st from left-hand side of chart 1, so ending with a k row.
Joining row (wrong side) With A, p across 21 sts of second piece, then p across 21 sts on holder. *42 sts.*
Beg with a k row, work remaining 15 chart rows. Bind off all sts.

LETTER "O"
With A, cast on 42 sts.
Beg with a k row, work 10 rows in St st from chart 2 (see page 138).
Divide for center hole
Next row (right side) K21 sts, turn and cont on these sts only, leaving rem 21 sts on a spare needle.
Beg with a p row, work 24 rows from right-hand side of chart 2, so ending with a k row.
Leave sts on a holder.
Rejoin B yarn to sts on spare needle and k to end.
Beg with a p row, work 24 rows from right-hand side of chart 2, so ending with a k row.
Joining row (wrong side) With A, p across 21 sts of second piece, then p across 21 sts on holder. *42 sts.*
Beg with a k row, work remaining 15 chart rows. Bind off all sts.

LETTER "E"
With A, cast on 21 sts and work 94 rows in St st from main strip chart 4 (see page 140).
With A, cast on 14 sts and work 21 rows in St st from center strip chart 5.

LETTER "L"
With A, cast on 21 sts and work 51 rows in St st from chart 3 (see page 138).
Bind off.

CHART 1 (N)

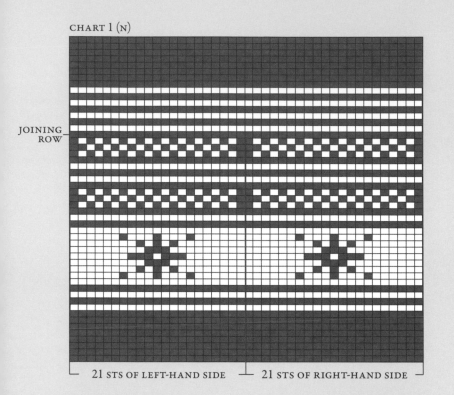

JOINING ROW

⌐ 21 STS OF LEFT-HAND SIDE ⌐ 21 STS OF RIGHT-HAND SIDE ⌐

TO FINISH

Cut out two pieces of cardboard for each letter, using the templates on pages 140 and 141. Cut out one piece of red felt for each letter, adding a ⅝in allowance all around. Making sure you work with each letter in reverse, place the felt on one piece of cardboard, fold the allowance over onto the back, and attach it all around with double-sided tape. When working the upper part of the "e," cut a small hole and clip around it so that the felt can be turned to the back more easily. Place the knitted pieces on the right side of the second cardboard template for each letter, and attach the excess fabric to the back of the cardboard with double-sided tape, stretching and easing to fit as necessary. When working the "e," first wrap the center bar with the knitted center strip, then wrap the remaining section with the main strip and slipstitch where they join. For each letter, place the wrong sides of the cardboards together and slipstitch around the edges.

CHART 2 (O)

CHART 3 (L)

KEY
■ A sage green
□ B ecru

138

CHART 4 (E—MAIN STRIP)

CHART 5 (E—CENTER STRIP)

KEY

■ A sage green

□ B ecru

14 STS

21 STS

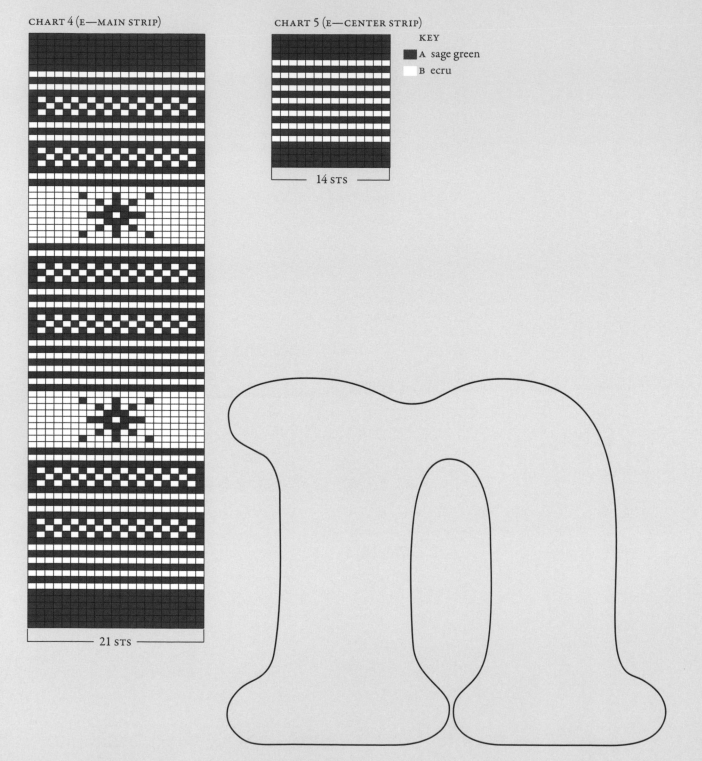

Hot-water bottle cover

As winter draws in and the days become shorter, who doesn't love snuggling up of an evening under the comforter with a warming hot-water bottle. This protective cover will stop you from getting scalded and help the hot-water bottle retain its heat for longer. The simple drawstring shape of the cover means it is easy to knit as there is no need for any tricky shaping.

SIZE
To fit a standard-sized hot-water bottle

MATERIALS
Debbie Bliss Cashmerino Aran (55% merino wool, 33% microfiber, 12% cashmere, approx 99 yd per 1¾oz/50g ball)
Two balls in stone
Pair each of sizes 6 and 8 knitting needles
12in of satin ribbon, ½in wide

GAUGE
22 sts and 24 rows to 4in square over patt (unstretched) using size 8 needles.

ABBREVIATIONS
See page 10.

TIP
You will need to insert the hot-water bottle into the cover before filling.

FRONT
With size 8 needles, cast on 43 sts.
1st row (right side) [P1, k1] 3 times, * p2, k1, p1, k1, p2, [k1, p1] twice, k1; rep from * to last st, p1.
2nd and every foll wrong-side row K all k sts and p all p sts as they appear.
3rd row P1, [k1, p1] to end.
5th row Rep 1st row.
7th row [K1, p1] twice, k1, * p2, [k1, p1] twice, k1, p2, k1, p1, k1; rep from * to last 2 sts, p1, k1.
9th row Rep 3rd row.
11th row Rep 7th row.
12th row Rep 2nd row.
These 12 rows **form** the front patt and are repeated 5 times more.
Change to size 6 needles.
Work 1st–4th rows once.
Eyelet row (right side) P1, k1, yo, k2tog, p1, k1, p1, yo, skp, p1, k1, p1, yo, k2tog, p1, k1, p1, yo, p2tog, [p1, k1] twice, p1, p2tog, yo, p1, k1, p1, skp, yo, p1, k1, p1, k2tog, yo, p1, k1, p1, skp, yo, k1, p1.
Next row [K1, p1] 3 times, * k2, p1, k1, p1, k2, [p1, k1] twice, p1; rep from * to last st, k1.
Change to size 8 needles.

Work 7th–12th rows once.
Work 1st–4th rows once more.
Bind off in patt.

BACK
With size 8 needles, cast on 43 sts.
[Work 7th–12th rows as given for Front.
Work 1st–12th rows as given for Front] 5 times, then work 1st–6th rows once more.
Change to size 6 needles.
Work 7th–10th rows once more.
Eyelet row K1, p1, k1, yo, skp, p2, k1, yo, k2tog, p1, k1, p1, yo, skp, p1, k1, p1, yo, k2tog, p1, k1, p1, skp, yo, p1, k1, p1, k2tog, yo, p1, k1, p1, skp, yo, k1, p2, k2tog, yo, k1, p1, k1.
Next row [P1, k1] twice, p1, * k2, [p1, k1] twice, p1, k2, p1, k1, p1; rep from * to last 2 sts, k1, p1.
Work 1st–10th row once more.
Bind off in patt.

TO FINISH
Sew together the two pieces around cast-on and side edges, leaving top edge open. Thread ribbon through the eyelets and tie at center front.

Christmas tree decorations

Add some sparkle to the yuletide season with these beaded tree-shaped Christmas decorations; use them either as alternative ornaments for the Christmas tree or alongside the traditional decorations, garland, and holiday trinkets. Made in three separate sections and then sewn together to form the different branches of the fir tree, the beads are added on in the final stage to mimic festive ornaments.

SIZE
Approximately 2¾in x 3in, excluding ribbon loop

MATERIALS
Debbie Bliss Baby Cashmerio (55% merino wool, 33% micro-fiber, 12% cashmere, approx 99 yd per 1¾oz/50g ball)
Small amount in each of red, white, and dark green
Pair of size 2 knitting needles
12in of narrow ribbon for each tree
Assorted beads

GAUGE
28 sts and 56 rows to 4in square over garter st using size 2 needles.

ABBREVIATIONS
s2togkp slip 2 sts together, k1, pass 2 slipped sts over.
Also see page 10.

LOWER SECTION
With size 2 needles, cast on 43 sts and k 2 rows.
Next row (right side) K9, [k2tog] twice, k17, [k2tog] twice, k9. *39 sts.*
K 1 row.
Next row K8, [k2tog] twice, k15, [k2tog] twice, k8. *35 sts.*
K 1 row.
** **Next row** K7, [k2tog] twice, k13, [k2tog] twice, k7. *31 sts.*
K 1 row.
Next row K6, [k2tog] twice, k11, [k2tog] twice, k6. *27 sts.*
K 1 row.
*** **Next row** K5, [k2tog] twice, k9, [k2tog] twice, k5. *23 sts.*
K 1 row.
Next row K4, [k2tog] twice, k7, [k2tog] twice, k4. *19 sts.*
K 1 row.
Next row K3, [k2tog] twice, k5, [k2tog] twice, k3. *15 sts.*
K 1 row.
Next row K2, [k2tog] twice, k3, [k2tog] twice, k2. *11 sts.*

K 1 row.
Next row K1, [k2tog] twice, k1, [k2tog] twice, k1. *7 sts.*
K 1 row.
Next row K2tog, s2togkp, k2tog. *3 sts.*
K 1 row.
Next row S2togkp and fasten off.

CENTER SECTION
With size 2 needles, cast on 35 sts and k 2 rows.
Work as Lower Section from ** to end.

UPPER SECTION
With size 2 needles, cast on 27 sts and k 2 rows.
Work as Lower Section from *** to end.

TO FINISH
Sew back seam in each section. Thread a length of ribbon up through the tip of each section, then leaving a loop of ribbon at the top of the upper section, thread the ribbon back through and tie the two ends together inside the lower section to secure. Sew beads to each section for tree decorations.

145

Christmas stocking

Worked in festive red and white, this Christmas stocking is knitted in stockinette stitch. The majority of the stocking has been kept plain, with the decorative colorwork stripes and snowflake motifs kept to a minimum. While it is small and simple enough to knit up in double-quick time, this stocking is big enough to hold all your surprise gifts and goodies.

SIZE
Approximately 18in long

MATERIALS
Debbie Bliss Rialto Aran
(100% extra-fine merino wool,
approx 88 yd per 1¾oz/50g
ball)
Two balls in red (A) and one
ball in ecru (B)
Pair each of sizes 7 and 8
knitting needles
8in of ribbon for hanging loop

GAUGE
18 sts and 24 rows to 4in
square over St st using size
8 needles.

ABBREVIATIONS
See page 10.

TO MAKE
With size 7 needles and A, cast on 65 sts.
K 1 row A, [k 2 rows B, k 2 rows A] twice, k 2 rows B.
Change to size 8 needles.
Beg with a k row, work 4 rows in St st in A.
Cont in St st and work 27 rows from chart 1 (see page 148).
Beg with a p row, work 30 rows in St st in A only.
Change to size 7 needles.
P 1 row.
Shape heel
First side
Next 2 rows K4, turn, sl 1, p3.
Next 2 rows K6, turn, sl 1, p5.
Next 2 rows K8, turn, sl 1, p7.
Cont to work shortened turning rows in this way until you have worked: K22, turn, sl 1, p21.
Next 2 rows K18, turn, sl 1, p17.
Next 2 rows K14, turn, sl 1, p13.

Next 2 rows K10, turn, sl 1, p9.
Next 2 rows K6, turn, sl 1, p5.
K 1 row across all sts.
Second side
Next 2 rows P4, turn, sl 1, k3.
Next 2 rows P6, turn, sl 1, k5.
Next 2 rows P8, turn, sl 1, k7.
Cont to work shortened turning rows in this way until you have worked: P22, turn, sl 1, k21.
Next 2 rows P18, turn, sl 1, k17.
Next 2 rows P14, turn, sl 1, k13.
Next 2 rows P10, turn, sl 1, k9.
Next 2 rows P6, turn, sl 1, k5.
Beg with a p row, work 5 rows in St st across all sts.
Change to size 8 needles.
Beg with a k row, work 9 rows in St st from chart 2 (see page 148).
Change to size 7 needles and work in A only.
Beg with a p row, work 7 rows in St st.

CHART 1

CHART 2

KEY

■ A red
□ B ecru

Shape toe
Next row (right side) K2, ssk, k25, k2tog, k3, ssk, k25, k2tog, k2.
Work 3 rows in St st.
Next row K2, ssk, k23, k2tog, k3, ssk, k23, k2tog, k2.
Work 3 rows in St st.
Cont in stripes of 2 rows B, 2 rows A alternately as follows:
Next row With B, k2, ssk, k21, k2tog, k3, ssk, k21, k2tog, k2.
P 1 row in B.
Work 2 rows in St st in A.
Next row With B, k2, ssk, k19, k2tog, k3, ssk, k19, k2tog, k2.
P 1 row in B.
Next row With A, k2, ssk, k17, k2tog, k3, ssk, k17, k2tog, k2.
P 1 row in A.
Next row With B, k2, ssk, k15, k2tog, k3, ssk,

k15, k2tog, k2.
P 1 row in B.
Cut off B and cont in A only.
Next row K2, ssk, k13, k2tog, k3, ssk, k13, k2tog, k2.
Next row P2, p2tog, p11, p2tog tbl, p3, p2tog, k11, p2tog tbl, p2.
Next row K2, ssk, k9, k2tog, k3, ssk, k9, k2tog, k2.
Next row P2, p2tog, p7, p2tog tbl, p3, p2tog, k7, p2tog tbl, p2.
Next row K2, ssk, k5, k2tog, k3, ssk, k5, k2tog, k2.
Bind off.

TO FINISH
Sew toe and back seam, matching patts and stripes. Fold ribbon in half to form a loop and sew inside the top of the stocking.

Laced-edged pillow
Perk up a plain pillowcase with a decorative lace edging. Some lace patterns can be challenging, but not this one as it is worked over just 6 stitches and a 4-row repeat. Knitted widthwise, the edging can be made as short or long as you like, so it can be used to trim any size of pillow. Worked in my Eco Baby, the organic cotton yarn gives the lace extra crispness and clarity of stitch.

SIZE
1¼in wide at widest point

MATERIALS
Debbie Bliss Eco Baby (100% organic cotton, approx 137 yd per 1¾oz/50g ball)
One ball in white
Pair of size 3 knitting needles
One small pillowcase

GAUGE
25 sts and 34 rows to 4in square over St st using size 3 needles.

ABBREVIATIONS
yo2 yarn over twice (yarn around right-hand needle twice to make 2 new sts).
Also see page 10.

TO MAKE
With size 3 needles, cast on 6 sts.
1st row (right side) K1, k2tog, yo, k2, yo2, k1.
2nd row K2, k1 tbl, k2tog, yo, k3.
3rd row K1, k2tog, yo, k5.
4th row Bind off 2 sts, with 1 st on needle after bind-off, k2tog, yo, k3.
These 4 rows **form** the patt and are repeated.
Cont in patt until edging fits around the pillowcase approximately ¾in in from outer edge, allowing extra to ease at each corner, ending with a 3rd patt row. Bind off knitwise.

TO FINISH
Sew together cast-on and bound-off edges of edging, then beginning at one corner, hand stitch the edging in place, easing in when turning the corners.

lovely lace pillow
for sweet dreams

Collared scarf

This combination of both a scarf and a collar rolled into one makes a clever fashion accessory. Worked in seed stitch—the perfect reversible fabric—it can be worn either as it is or tucked inside a neck opening for extra warmth. This scarf is knitted in Cashmerino Aran for absolute comfort and softness.

SIZE
Approximately 5¼in x 46in

MATERIALS
Debbie Bliss Cashmerino Aran (55% merino wool, 33% microfiber, 12% cashmere, approx 99 yd per 1¾oz/50g ball)
Three balls in stone
Pair of size 8 knitting needles
One button

GAUGE
18 sts and 32 rows to 4in square over seed st using size 8 needles.

ABBREVIATIONS
yo2 yarn over twice (yarn around right-hand needle twice to make 2 new sts).
Also see page 10.

TO MAKE
With size 8 needles, cast on 25 sts.
Seed st row K1, [p1, k1] to end.
Seed st 99 rows more.
Next row Bind off 10 sts, seed st to end.
Seed st one row.
Next row Cast on 12 sts, seed st to end.
Seed st 170 rows.
Next row Bind off 12 sts, seed st to end.
Next row Seed st to end, turn.
Next row Cast on 10 sts, seed st to end.
Seed st 24 rows.
Buttonhole row Seed st 12, k2tog, yo2, ssk, seed st to end.
Next row Seed st to end, working [k1, p1 tbl] into yo2.
Seed st 74 rows.
Bind off.
Sew on button.

a perfect plum
pudding baby's hat

Christmas baby hat

Get in the festive mood by knitting up this cute baby's hat with a rolled brim. Worked in an aran-weight yarn, there are only a few rows that involve a color change so it is simpler to knit than it may appear. A white topping, picot-edged leaves, and bobble berries make the hat look like the traditional British Christmas dessert—plum pudding.

SIZES
To fit ages 3–6 (6–12) months

MATERIALS
Debbie Bliss Rialto Aran (100% extra-fine merino wool, approx 99 yd per 1¾oz/50g ball)
One ball in each of chocolate (M) and ecru (C)
Debbie Bliss Baby Cashmerino (55% merino wool, 33% microfiber, 12% cashmere, approx 137 yd per 1¾oz/50g ball)
Small amount in each of dark green for leaves and red for berries
Pair each of sizes 3, 6, and 8 knitting needles

GAUGE
18 sts and 24 rows to 4in square over St st using size 8 needles.

ABBREVIATIONS
pwise purlwise
Also see page 10.

NOTE
When working with two colors, either use separate strands of yarn for each color area, twisting yarns at color change to avoid holes, or weave yarn not in use across wrong side where necessary in order to avoid long yarn floats.

TO MAKE
With size 6 needles and M, cast on 73 (81) sts.
Beg with a k row, work 12 rows in St st.
Change to size 8 needles.
Beg with a k row, work 22 (26) rows in St st.
Cont in St st and work in patt as follows (see NOTE):
Next row (right side) K 15 (17)M, 1C, 15 (17)M, 2C, 16 (18)M, 1C, 17 (19)M, 1C, 5M.
Next row P 4M, 3C, 4 (5)M, 1C, 11M, 1 (2)C, 6 (7)M, 1C, 8 (9)M, 3C, 8M, 1C, 6 (8)M, 2C, 3 (4)M, 1 (2)C, 10M.
Next row K 4M, 1C, 4 (5)M, 3C, 1 (2)M, 3C, 5 (7)M, 4C, 5M, 5C, 6M, 3 (4)C, 4 (5)M, 3 (4)C, 4 (3)M, 1C, 4 (5)M, 3C, 3 (4)M, 4C, 3M.
Next row P 2M, 6C, 1M, 5 (6)C, 2 (3)M, 3C, 2 (1)M, 5 (6)C, 2M, 5 (7)C, 3 (4)M, 8 (7)C, 3M, 6 (7)C, 3 (4)M, 8 (10)C, 3M, 3C, 3M.
Next row K2M, 5C, 1M, 10 (13)C, 1M, 19 (20)C, 1M, 34 (21)C, 0 (1)M, 0 (16)C.
Cont in C only.
P 1 row.
Dec row K1 (0), [k2tog, k7] 8 (9) times. *65 (72) sts.*
P 1 row.
Dec row K1 (0), [k2tog, k6] 8 (9) times. *57 (63) sts.*
P 1 row.
Dec row K1 (0), [k2tog, k5] 8 (9) times. *49 (54) sts.*
P 1 row.
Dec row K1 (0), [k2tog, k4] 8 (9) times. *41 (46) sts.*
P 1 row.
Dec row K1, [k2tog, k3] 8 (9) times. *33 (37) sts.*
Dec row [P2, p2tog] 8 (9) times, p1. *25 (28) sts.*
Next row K1 (0), [k2tog] to end. *13 (14) sts.*

Next row P1 (0), [p2tog] to end. *7 sts.*
Leaving a 16in yarn tail, cut off yarn, thread
through rem sts, pull to gather, and secure. Sew
seam, reversing seam at lower edge to allow the
hem to roll up.

LEAVES (MAKE 3)
With size 3 needles and dark green, cast on
21 sts.
Beg with a k row, work 4 rows in St st.
Picot row K1, [yo, k2tog] to end.
Beg with a p row, work 4 rows in St st.
Work bind-off as follows:
With right-hand needle, pick up the first st of
the cast-on row, place it on left-hand needle
and k tog with first st on left-hand needle, place
next st from cast-on edge on left-hand needle
and k tog with next st on needle, take first st
on right-hand needle over second to bind off;
binding off sts in this way, cont to k each st tog
with corresponding st of cast-on edge and bind
off all sts.
Fold in half and sew straight edges together.

BERRIES (MAKE 3)
With size 3 needles and red, cast on 1 st.
Next row [K1, p1, k1, p1, k1] all into st. *5 sts.*
K 1 row.
P 1 row.
Rep last 2 rows once more.
Next row K2tog, k1, k2tog. *3 sts.*
Next row Slip 1 pwise, p2tog, psso, and
fasten off.
With a blunt-ended yarn needle, work a run-
ning stitch around edge of berry, pull to gather
into a bobble, and secure.

TO FINISH
Attach three leaves to the top of the hat and sew
the berries in place to the center.

Yarn Suppliers

For suppliers of Debbie Bliss yarns please contact:

USA

Knitting Fever Inc.
315 Bayview Avenue
Amityville
NY 11701, USA
t: +1 516 546 3600
w: www.knittingfever.com

CANADA

Diamond Yarns Ltd.
155 Martin Ross Avenue
Unit 3
Toronto
Ontario M3J 2L9, Canada
t: +1 416 736 6111
w: www.diamondyarn.com

UK & WORLDWIDE DISTRIBUTORS

Designer Yarns Ltd.
Units 8–10
Newbridge Industrial Estate
Pitt Street, Keighley
W. Yorkshire BD21 4PQ, UK
t: +44 (0) 1535 664222
e: alex@designeryarns.uk.com
w: www.designeryarns.uk.com

MEXICO

Estambres Crochet SA de CV
Aaron Saenz 1891–7
Col. Santa Maria, Monterrey
N.L. 64650, Mexico
t: +52 (81) 8335 3870
e: abremer@redmundial.com.mx

BELGIUM/NETHERLANDS

Pavan
Thomas Van Theemsche
Meerlaanstraat 73
9860 Balegem (Oostrezele)
Belgium
t: +32 (0) 9 221 85 94
e: pavan@pandora.be

DENMARK

Fancy Knit
Hovedvejen 71
8586 Oerum Djurs
Ramten, Denmark
t: +45 59 46 21 89
e: roenneburg@mail.dk

FINLAND

Eiran Tukku
Mäkelänkatu 54 B
00510 Helsinki, Finland
t: +358 50 346 0575
e: maria.hellbom@eirantukku.fi
w: www.eirantukku.fi

FRANCE

Laines Plassard
La Filature
71800 Varennes-sous-Dun
France
t: +33 (0) 3 8528 2828
w: www.laines-plassard.com

GERMANY/AUSTRIA/ SWITZERLAND/ LUXEMBOURG

Designer Yarns (Deutschland) GmbH
Welserstraße 10g
D-51149 Köln, Germany
t: +49 (0) 2203 1021910
e: info@designeryarns.de
w: www.designeryarns.de

ICELAND

Storkurinn ehf
Laugavegi 59
101 Reykjavík, Iceland
t: +354 551 8258
e: storkurinn@simnet.is

SPAIN

Oyambre Needlework SL
Balmes, 200 At. 4
08006 Barcelona, Spain
t: +34 (0) 93 487 26 72
e: info@oyambronline.com

SWEDEN

Nysta garn och textil
Hogasvagen 20
S-131 47 Nacka, Sweden
t: +46 (0) 8 612 0330
e: nina@nysta.se
w: www.nysta.se

RUSSIA

Golden Fleece
Soloviyny proczd 16
117593 Moscow, Russia
t: +8 (903) 000 1967
e: natalya@rukodelie.ru
w: www.rukodelie.ru

POLAND

Art-Bijou os
Krakowiakow 5/31
31-962 Krakow, Poland
e: kontakt@artbijou.com

AUSTRALIA/NEW ZEALAND

Prestige Yarns Pty Ltd.
P.O. Box 39, Bulli
NSW 2516, Australia
t: +61 (0) 2 4285 6669
e: info@prestigeyarns.com
w: www.prestigeyarns.com

HONG KONG

East Unity Company Ltd.
Unit B2
7/F Block B
Kailey Industrial Centre
12 Fung Yip Street
Chan Wan
t: (852) 2869 7110
e: eastunity@yahoo.com.hk

TAIWAN

U-Knit
1F, 199-1 Sec
Zhong Xiao East Road
Taipei, Taiwan
t: +886 2 27527557
e: shuindigo@hotmail.com

THAILAND

Needle World Co Ltd
Pradit Manoontham Road
Bangkok 10310
t: 662 933 9167
e: needle-world.coltd@google-mail.com

BRAZIL

Quatro Estacoes Com
Las Linhas e Acessorios Ltda
Av. Das Nacoes Unidas
12551-9 Andar
Cep 04578-000 Sao Paulo
Brazil
t: +55 11 3443 7736
e: cristina@4estacoeslas.com.br

For more information on my other books and yarns, please visit www.debbieblissonline.com

Acknowledgments

This book wouldn't have been possible without the generous collaboration of the following:

Rosy Tucker, who—as I mentioned in my introduction—played such as important part in producing so many of the projects in this book.

Penny Hill, for her essential pattern compiling and organizing the knitters.

Jane O'Shea, Lisa Pendreigh, and Katherine Case at Quadrille Publishing for being such a wonderful team to work with.

Mia Pejcinovic for the perfect styling and overall look.

Penny Wincer for the beautiful photography.

The knitters, for the huge effort they put into creating perfect knits under deadline pressure: Cynthia Brent, Barbara Clapham, Pat Church, Jacqui Dunt, Shirley Kennet, Maisie Lawrence, and Frances Wallace.

My fantastic agent, Heather Jeeves.

The distributors, agents, retailers, and knitters who support all my books and yarns with such enthusiasm and, once again, make what I do possible.

First published in the United States of America
In 2010 by **Trafalgar Square Books**
North Pomfret, Vermont 05053

Printed in China

Originally published in the United Kingdom in 2010
By Quadrille Publishing Limited, London.

Text and project designs © 2010 Debbie Bliss
Photography, design, and layout © 2010 Quadrille Publishing Ltd

Editorial Director Jane O'Shea
Creative Director Helen Lewis
Project Editor Lisa Pendreigh
Designer Katherine Case
Photographer Penny Wincer
Stylist Mia Pejcinovic
Pattern Checker Rosy Tucker
Pattern Illustrator Bridget Bodoano
Production Director Vincent Smith
Production Controller Ruth Deary

ISBN: 978-1-57076-461-5

Library of Congress Control Number:
2010926721

10 9 8 7 6 5 4 3 2 1

First Edition